INSIGHT

G000153772

RHODES

APA PUBLICATIONS

Part of the Langenscheidt Publishing Group

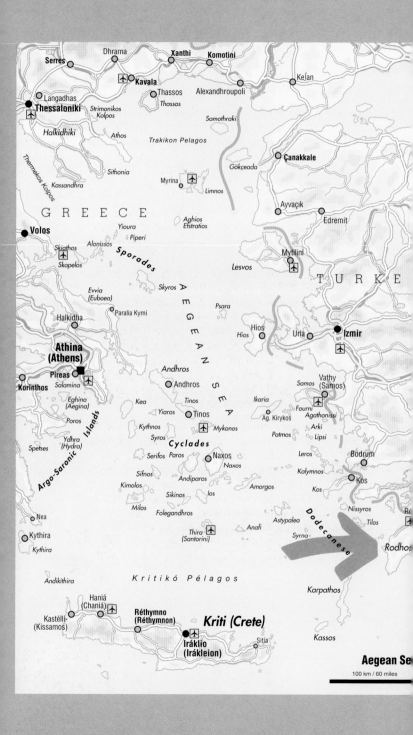

Welcome!

This guidebook combines the interests and enthusiasms of two of the world's best-known information providers: Insight Guides, who have set the standard for visual travel guides since 1970, and Discovery Channel, the world's premier source of non-fiction television programming.

In the following pages Insight Guides' correspondent on Rhodes, the sunniest and largest island of the Dodecanese, has created a selection of itineraries grouped around the island's four key bases: Rhodes City, Arhángelos, Líndhos and Gennadio. Designed to suit a variety of tastes and time frames, they include all the favourite sights but also many hidden gems that only someone intimately acquainted with Rhodes is likely to know – quiet beaches, remote monasteries and semi-wild archaeological sites. One of the author's aims has been to show how visitors can genuinely come into contact with the land and its people. Whatever your tastes, this guide shows you how to get the most from this justly popular destination.

 Susanne Heidelck is a writer who has lived on Rhodes for over 15 years. She claims her move to the island wasn't an easy transition. Though confident that she would cope well with whatever life there would bring, she says it wasn't until she began to love both the island and its people that she felt anything like equal to the task. To this day she frequently feels like an honoured guest who receives more from her hosts than she will ever be able to give.

C O N T E N T S

Pages 2/3: twilight over the port of Rhodes City

Líndhos

Gennadio

Pages 8/9: fishing boat bow

A History of Foreign Occupation

'In answer to our query about which had been the best of all the
occupying powers, up to the present day, the old salt scratched his
head and replied that, actually, there had not been any great dif-
ferences between them. The main thing was to be occupied, spared
from independence, which would only bring higher taxes.'

from *The Seasick Whale* by Ephraim Kishon

There is scarcely a more laconic commentary on the history of much-
occupied Rhodes than that of the fisherman netted by Israeli hu-
morist Ephraim Kishon. Of course, Rhodes has long been and
remains subject to foreign occupation, whether by Turkish Janis-
saries, who held the fortress walls for three centuries, Italian fas-
cists, who propelled the island into World War II or, indeed, by
the present-day hordes who roam the narrow alleyways of the Old
Town in revealing shorts and halter-neck tops – the 'uniform' of
the latest conquerors. It is indicative of the specifically Rhodian
mentality that the locals have adjusted to even this latest, and
perhaps most insidious, invasion. From the Ottoman turban to
the German helmet, from the leather loincloth to the rattling suit
of knightly armour, the inhabitants of this island have, of course,
seen everything.

   The sun-drenched silhouette of the capital city stands as an impressive testament to its many and varied foreign masters. With its
minarets, cupolas and church steeples, its imposing Palace of the
Grand Masters and mighty fortified ramparts, Rhodes City displays
its history on its skyline. All this is outshone, however – and shone
down upon – by the one to whom this island has always owed its
first allegiance: the sun-god, Helios.

Culture

Of course, what dry modern science has surmised, the Greeks have known for centuries. It was Helios who brought the island to his father Zeus's attention when it suddenly popped up during the first tertiary period. As a result, he received the island as a gift and, in gratitude, decided to shower Rhodes with sunshine in perpetuity. The consequences of this particular 'occupation' were abundant harvests, wealth and a booming economy.

In antiquity, the island of Rhodes was a bustling trade centre with business connections throughout the entire Mediterranean region. Wine, wheat and oil found international markets as export goods, and great trading houses from Mesopotamia to Egypt maintained agencies in the city of Líndhos, which at that time experienced a renaissance of cultural and economic growth. 'Ten Rhodians, ten ships,' was the saying. In other words, whoever lived on Rhodes was automatically considered wealthy.

The inhabitants of the island probably owed their wealth as much to the fact that they didn't go around senselessly swinging their swords as they did to the blessings of Helios. Skilled diplomats from the outset, they understood how to maintain what was a precarious but at any rate largely independent perch between the big power blocs of the day. In times of crisis, they actually allowed themselves to be occupied and then made the best of it. Only if the conditions set by the conquerors seemed exceedingly harsh would they defend themselves tooth and nail. Uncharacteristically, perhaps, they participated in the Trojan War. Apparently, it represented an opportunity to gain prestige.

In 408BC, the three extremely rich municipalities of Kamíros, Ialyssós and Líndhos decided to found a city whose location would provide the best possible guarantee against encroachment from the east: Rhodes City. A street grid was designed according to the most

11

modern architectural standards of the time which, in its rectilinear structure, is still visible today. Rhodes City rapidly consolidated its position as capital city and spiritual and economic centre of the island. Cicero, Caesar and Tiberius were students at its famous School of Rhetoric; ships from East and West passed through its harbour. An immense number of statues were erected to adorn the new metropolis, the inhabitants of which still numbered some 100,000 at the turn of the first millennium – a population density which has never again been matched.

However, from the date of unification with Rome – seen from today's vantage as a great tactical error – the gradual decline of the city began. The island was incorporated as a Roman province of the rising power. Now Rhodes provided its wine at a ridiculously low price to supply the disdainful and decadent imperial court, and was forced to make large deliveries.

Furthermore, earthquakes constantly shook the land and epidemics reduced the population, weakening the island's defences towards the growing danger from the East. In AD515 Rhodes City was completely destroyed by an earthquake. The city built after the cataclysm corresponded in size to the Old Town of today. Drawn into the Byzantine Empire, Rhodes had to defend itself repeatedly through the centuries against the advancing charges of the Persians and Saracens. Many of the events of that period are shrouded in darkness. The curtain rises again in the year 1082, when two new occupying powers appeared on the busy Mediterranean stage: Venice and Genoa.

It was thanks to the Genoans that Rhodes fell into the hands of the Crusaders. In some fierce horse trading, a Genoan admiral (in reality a pirate), bartered away the entire island to the knights, who proceeded to make Rhodes their base for the next two centuries. For the purposes of the holy wars, and as the last strategic staging point before Constantinople, Rhodes had all sorts of strategic advantages. What started out as an offensive campaign against the Turks soon degenerated into a war of defence, which is reflected in the increasingly impregnable fortifications which the knights erected on the island over the years. But neither cannons nor double walls were

12

finally able to stop the inexorable approach of the Ottomans. Some 70 years after the sack of Constantinople, Rhodes City fell. On 22 December 1522, the Grand Master, Villiers de l'Île Adam, had to capitulate with scarcely 200 men remaining to him. Sultan Suleiman I promised him and his people an honourable departure, and the majority of Rhodes' Greek population followed the departing Crusaders into exile. Remaining Rhodians who had fought alongside the knights were slaughtered, while others capitulated. They looked on as Christian churches were turned into mosques, and accepted the taxes which were levied to finance the Turkish administration. Since they were forbidden to set foot inside the capital after sunset, they settled outside the walls. On the ground plan of the ancient, spaciously planned city, the present day city, with its tangled network of streets, was overlaid.

Medieval fortifications ring the Old Town

View over the roofs of the Old Town

By and large, the indigenous population adjusted well to Ottoman rule. It wasn't until the 19th century that the Turks' hold on the island began to slip, as all over Greece rebellions rose up against the ruling dynasty. The Ottomans' response was reactionary. From 1874 on, they clamped down on trade, suspended religious freedom, and resorted to violent means in order to quell revolt. However, the course of history could not be altered and, by 1912, the Turks had been deposed by the Italians.

Once more the face of the island's capital underwent substantial alterations. Huge and pompous neoclassical buildings, which bring to mind the Via Nazionale in Rome, sprang up. But though in the years 1922 to 1943, and particularly during the Fascist era, large tracts of land were expropriated, the Italians did much for the development of the island. Donkey paths were paved and the Palace of the Grand Masters, destroyed in an explosion, was reconstructed. Even today, a marble plaque still hangs there, paying homage to Benito Mussolini. Many buildings were renovated during the Italian occupation, although it could be said that they were not beautified nor, strictly speaking, preserved. Rhodes, viewed by the Italians primarily as a vacation home for Axis dignitaries, can still look back with pride to many of the achievements of that period.

After the surrender of the Italians to the Allied forces in 1943, Rhodes became the site of many bitter battles which led at last to the final capitulation of the Germans in 1945. Up to the year 1947, the island remained under the command of the British, who restored order to the chaotic administrative apparatus. In 1948, Rhodes became part of Greece.

Historical Highlights

4000BC First human settlements on the island.

2500 Settlement by the Minoans.

1600 Rhodes' Mycenaean Period; settled by the Ahaians, who found Líndhos, Kamíros and Ialyssós.

1200 The Trojan War.

1100 Beginning of the Dorian migration. The Dorians divide the island into three areas with capitals in Líndhos, Kamíros and Ialyssós.

1000–700 Formation of the six-city Dodecanese league, Hexapolis.

650 First Rhodian colonies on Sicily, Italy, Spain and France.

490 First Persian War. Rhodes is compelled to fight for the Persians. Greek victory at Marathon.

480 Second Persian War. Greek victory in the Battle of Salamis.

478 Rhodes joins Delian League.

408 Founding of the new capital, Rhodes City. Period of cultural and economic ascendancy.

336 Alexander the Great of Macedonia occupies Kós. Rhodes joins him against Persia.

331 Alexandria is founded. It becomes a vital trading partner.

323 Alexander's generals divide the conquered areas, leading to war. Rhodes allies with Egypt.

305 The Macedonian, Dhemetrios Poliokretes, lays siege to Rhodes for a year without success. The Colossus of Rhodes, a 34-m (111-ft 6in) bronze statue, is erected.

304 Rhodes establishes first relations with Rome.

227 Earthquake. The Colossus is demolished.

201 Philip of Macedonia occupies Rhodian possessions in Asia Minor. Rhodes asks Rome for help.

190 Rhodes joins Rome against Hannibal. Victory for Rome.

164 Alliance pact with Rome.

42 Cassius completely destroys the City of Rhodes and the fleet.

AD50 St Paul lands at Líndhos.

395 Rhodes becomes a province of the Eastern Roman Empire.

1125 Venice conquers Rhodes.

1306 Crusaders acquire Rhodes from a Genoan pirate. Great works by the Knights of St John.

1457–1522 Failed Turkish attempts to take over the city.

1522 Six-month siege by Turkey under Suleiman the Magnificent.

1523 The Knights of St John capitulate. Rhodes remains under Turkish hegemony until 1912.

1912 Rhodes occupied by Italy.

1943 The German Wehrmacht invades Rhodes.

1945 British and Greek commandos liberate Rhodes.

1948 Treaty ratified and Rhodes and Dodecanese become part of Greek state, 7 March, 1948.

1949 Greek Civil War between Communists and US-backed Government forces comes to an end.

1967 Coup by the right-wing Colonels leads to dictatorship under the Junta.

1974 Democracy restored after Junta falls over Cyprus troubles.

1981 First socialist government, PASOK, elected.

1983 Greece joins the EU.

1988 UNESCO declares the City of Rhodes a World Heritage Site.

1993 Rhodes celebrates the 2,400 year anniversary of the founding of Rhodos; PASOK re-elected.

1995 The 16 Mediterranean members of the World Tourism Organisation meet on Rhodes.

2000 PASOK narrowly re-elected under Kóstas Simítis.

2002 The euro replaces the Drachma.

Hippokrates Square in the Old Town

Beaches and Watermelons

With a surface area of 1,412km² (545 square miles), Rhodes is the largest of the Dodecanese archipelago which, despite its name (*dhód-heka* means 12), consists of 17 inhabited islands. Only 18km (11 miles) from the Turkish coast, Rhodes is the easternmost island in Europe, with the exception of the islet of Kastellórizo. From a geological point of view, the island should be considered part of the Turkish Taurus Massif. However, since 1948, Rhodes has been part of Greece, and Turkish speaking residents represent a small minority of the population. In addition to Greek, many elderly and even middle-aged Greeks speak Italian, which was the *lingua franca* during the occupation.

The distance from Cape Zonari – located on the 'nose' of the island, northeast of Rhodes City – down to Cape Prassoníssi in the extreme southwest is 80km (50 miles). The island has an average width of some 28km (17 miles). The 220km (137 miles) of coastline consist, for the most part, of sand and gravel beaches on the east coast; half beach, half rock in the west.

The tallest mountain peaks are, in the west, the 780m (2,560ft) high Proítis Ilías and the all but barren 1,215m (3986ft) high Attávyros; and in the east, the 825m (2,707ft) Akramitis.

The heavy forestation of Rhodes in comparison to other Greek islands is a result of the relatively high amount of rainfall it receives, mainly between November and April. The increasing cultivation of watermelons on the island uses up a large portion of the water available to communities, so there are occasional water shortages in the villages, especially after drier winters. However, the north coast, with its large hotel complexes, remains largely unaffected.

There is a stark contrast between the north – overloaded with hotels, restaurants and other businesses – and the south which is gemerally less visited by tourists and therefore largely orientated towards agriculture. Eighty percent of the commercial activity of the population is concentrated on only 10km² (4 square miles) of the island's surface area. Of the remaining area, approximately 17 percent is farmland; 32 percent pasture.

The New Economy

The history of Rhodes, which consists of an almost unbroken chain of foreign occupations, has made it easier for the populace to adjust to the modern variation on an old theme: tourism. Tourism has represented the main source of income on the island since the 1960s. Those farsighted enough to invest their money in land at that time were able to buy entire tracts of coast in the northwest of the island for a song. The policies of the Karamanlís government of the 1960s, although not always successful, did create the basis for a secure source of foreign exchange, from which the State received up to 25 percent profit. This remains an important source of income for the Greek Government.

Ninety percent of the tourism on the island consists of package tourism. Individual tourism barely enters the economic equation. However, Greece's neighbour, Turkey has become a serious competitor. In order to stop the charter tourists from wandering off to its more reasonably priced neighbour, Greece is trying to improve the services it offers visitors rather than impose restrictions on visits to Turkey, as it did in the past.

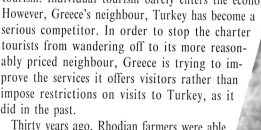

Thirty years ago, Rhodian farmers were able not only to feed the residents of their own island, but to export produce to the mainland and abroad. Today, fruit, vegetables, fish and meat must be imported. The broad range of EU wares now available even in the villages has been accompanied by price increases which poorer island residents cannot afford. Because of increased tobacco taxes, status symbols such as foreign cigarettes are no longer within the reach of this segment of the population. However, since the island gives the traveller the impression of prosperity, it can be difficult to grasp fully the insecurity of the majority of Rhodes' residents.

Rhodes (Rhodos)

4 km / 2.5 miles

Aegean Sea

Rodhos (Rhodes City)

Cape Zonari

Cape Vodhi
Kallithea
Cape Ladhiko

Thermes Kallithea
Koskinou
Asgourou
Rodhini
Kritika
Ixia
Tris
Trianda
Filerimos
Rastidha

FALIRAKI BEACH

M. Eleoussa
Kallithies
Maritsa
KOUMOULI

PSALIDHA

AFANDHOU

Cape Vagia

Kremasti
PARADHISS
Paradhissi
Dhamtria

Theologos (Tholos)
Epano Kalamos
Petaloudhes
M. Kalopetra

Afandhou

Loutani
Kolimbia
Moni Tsambika
TSAMBIKA
Stegna

PSINDHOS
Psindhos
Spilia
Arhipolis
Pikaria

Soroni
Plati
Fanes
Argiros

Dhimilia
Eleousa
MESSOVOUNA

Epta Pighés
Platanero
Arhangelos
Platania

Kalavardha

Dhimilia

M. Ag. Nikolaos Foundoukli

Makri
Malone

Ancient Kamiros
Cape Minas
Salakos
Kapi
PROFÍTIS ILIAS

Apollona
ASSOURI

Myrtonas
Nani

Mandhrikon

Embonas
Attaviros
1215

M. Artamiti

Kamiros Skala
Kritinia
AMARTOU

Kritinia Castle

MAKRI
STRONGILO ISLAND

Glyfadha Bay

ALIMNIA ISLAND
Cape Pounendi
TRAGOUSSA ISLAND

Rhodes City

Historical Rodhos

Rhodes City *(I Ródhos)* is the most recent urban settlement on the island. In contrast to ancient Líndhos, Kamíros and Ialyssós, the date of its construction can be pinpointed. In the year 408BC, the three older communities decided to found a city, the architectural plan of which was based on the theories held by the philosopher Hippodhamos. A short time after their construction the clear and distinctive road system, the well located port at the extreme northern tip of the island, and the Acropolis, amphitheatre and stadium, formed the heart of a significant culture. Rhodes City rose steadily in stature to become the island capital. In active cultural and economic exchange with Alexandria, the new Egyptian metropolis founded by Alexander the Great, a university came into being here, the library of which overshadowed even the world famous library of Alexandria. Education-hungry students from both the East and West, among them a large number of Roman emperors, came to study at ancient Rhodes.

However, the strategically desirable location did not bring growth, development and status without responsibility. Over the course of the subsequent turbulent centuries, it was the City of Rhodes which held out against attacks from the East.

The Palace of the Grand Masters

Rhodes City Today

Every year, millions of tourists flood through the narrow alleyways of the Old Town to visit the churches, museums and fortress walls, and familiarise themselves with the 2,400-year history of the island's capital. The surviving rich cultural mix etched graphically on the city's skyline in its architecture, which ranges from minarets to battlements, and the huge choice of holiday activities, not least its excellent beaches, make Rhodes an appealing destination for a wide range of visitors. During the day you can follow in the footsteps of the Knights of St John, admire Mycenaean archaeological finds, and visit

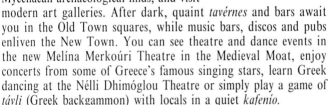

modern art galleries. After dark, quaint *tavérnes* and bars await you in the Old Town squares, while music bars, discos and pubs enliven the New Town. You can see theatre and dance events in the new Melína Merkoúri Theatre in the Medieval Moat, enjoy concerts from some of Greece's famous singing stars, learn Greek dancing at the Nélli Dhimóglou Theatre or simply play a game of *távli* (Greek backgammon) with locals in a quiet *kafenío*.

Over the course of the last 30 years, the city has accommodated the demands of package tourists with several thousand hotel beds. But not all the big new hotels are bland and impersonal, as is sometimes supposed. In the New Town and along the east and west coasts there is a selection of luxury and middle-level accommodation for discerning visitors. For example, the Rodos Imperial at Ixiá, is one of the most expensive hotels in Greece. Most of the new hotels have tennis courts and swimming pools, and all rooms are air-conditioned. (Independent travellers will have difficulties finding a room in these hotels during high season, but have a reasonable choice of budget and mid-range hotels.)

Alternatively, if you have a romantic side, you may like to rent one of the small pensions within the walls of the Old Town. While the rooms here tend to be cheaper and more basic, they often have a special view. Just after dawn, when other tourists are still asleep in their hotel-palaces outside the city walls, your own first glimpse out of the window will probably include a graceful palm tree, the cupola of a mosque, a plaza shaded by a plane tree or a peaceful interior courtyard resplendent with fuchsia, bougainvillaea and oleander. Before the shops open on **Odhós Sokrátous**, and the facades are obstructed by stridently coloured souvenirs, in one of the little plazas hidden away in the Old Town you may still experience a sense of what Rhodes was like before the invasion of the tourist hordes.

A Walk through the Old Town

Day tour: breakfast on Dhoriéos Square; Ibrahim Paşa Mosque; Square of Jewish Martyrs; lunch at the Plaka on Hippokrates Square; Greek coffee in a Turkish kafenío; a visit to a Turkish bath; the Suleiman Mosque and Turkish Library; the Palace of the Grand Masters; the Street of the Knights.

Odhós Sokrátous, the main thoroughfare of the Old Town, is invariably thronged with foreign visitors, particularly early–mid-morning. Their usual route is to proceed up the hill, swing off toward the Palace of the Grand Masters, making a quick raid on the Suleiman Mosque, and then return to Hippokrates Square via the Street of the Knights. Those wanting to avoid the crowds should visit this busy tourist street later in the day and take the tour outlined here, which takes a slightly different approach but still includes all the main attractions.

The tour begins with breakfast at the Oasis Restaurant, which is situated in one of the most beautiful squares of the Old Town, **Dhoriéos**. In the morning – an English breakfast is served from 9am – it is pleasantly tranquil here, and thanks to a gigantic plane tree, it is shady throughout the day. The square houses the striking **Mosque of Redjeb Paşa**, one of the most important mosques in the Old Town. Built in 1588 and set in peaceful gardens, it features a fountain made from Byzantine and medieval church columns and contains the sarcophagus of the Paşa.

In the surrounding alleys are small handicraft shops, cobblers, furriers and tailors' shops which have retained their traditional trades and identities. The beautiful **Ibrahim Paşa Mosque** on nearby Sofokleous St, built in 1531 and refurbished in 1928, has an exquisite interior and is the city's oldest Islamic house of worship. If the door is open, take a look inside. It is required that men wear long trousers if they enter the mosque. The pile of wooden sandals outside the entrance indicates that you should remove your shoes: here bare feet are obligatory.

With the help of the map in the wallet at the back of this guide, continue to the **Platía Evréon Martíron (Square of the Jewish Martyrs)** by way of Pythagora Street. The perplexing hodge-podge of alleys, dead ends, nooks and crannies in the medieval city contrasts sharply with the logical layout of the new quarter. However, it is evident on the ground that both sections of the city once formed an integrated whole: **Odhós Omírou, Odhós Aghíou Faníriou** and **Odhós Ippotón** (the Street of the Knights), still run along the

The Palace of the Masters

original grid of the ancient city designed 2,400 years ago by the geometrician Hippodhamus of Miletus.

The Square of the Jewish Martyrs, with its little sea horse fountains and shady plane trees, was once the centre of Evriaki, the Jewish Quarter. On Rhodes, Jews made up a significant community, whose position remained unthreatened even during the era of Italian fascism. Tragically, the invasion of the island by the German *Wehrmacht* during World War II initiated a systematic extermination of the congregation's membership, which once numbered 2,000. Only 35 of the mainly Sephardic Jews managed to survive. On the entrance gate of the synagogue, which is hidden on a side street, **Dhosiádhou**, you will find a plaque which names the local victims of the Holocaust. Those who are interested in further exploring the more recent history of the Old Town should walk from Platía Evréon Martíron to Pindharou where the majority of the houses are of postwar construction. In this area, the Holocaust extended not only to the people, but also to their homes.

Of course, the walls of the city hold much more than the memories of these recent atrocities. The picturesque capital of Rhodes has been coveted over the centuries by a string of ruthless conquerors, and what today appears to be the harmonious integration of a

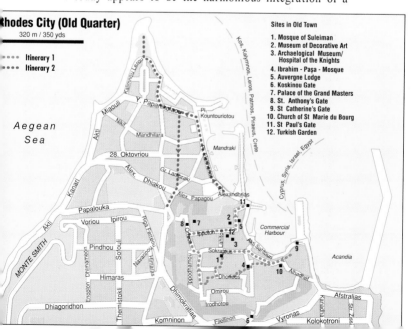

Rhodes City (Old Quarter)

320 m / 350 yds

- ●●●● Itinerary 1
- ●●●● Itinerary 2

Aegean Sea

Sites in Old Town

1. Mosque of Suleiman
2. Museum of Decorative Art
3. Archaelogical Museum/ Hospital of the Knights
4. Ibrahim - Paşa - Mosque
5. Auvergne Lodge
6. Koskinou Gate
7. Palace of the Grand Masters
8. St. Anthony's Gate
9. St Catherine's Gate
10. Church of St Marie du Bourg
11. St Paul's Gate
12. Turkish Garden

diverse variety of architectural styles and cultural elements is really the result of a chain of bloody wars and bitter defeats. Thus, the mosques were originally Crusader churches, which were purged of every representation of the human figure and then topped with minarets. Prior to this, however, the Knights of St John had 'renovated' Greek Orthodox churches, changing them into Roman Catholic cathedrals. One example is **Panaghía tou Kástro** (8am–7pm, closed Mon; admission charge) in Alexander the Great Square, which now houses the island's collection of Byzantine art.

If you continue through **Aristotelous Street** you come to **Hippokrates Square**, a focal point for tourist traffic. Here you can sit very comfortably, for a somewhat inflated price, and enjoy a view of the former civil courthouse, the Kastellania, which now serves a more sedate function and houses the library and Historical and Folklore Archive. Among the many fish restaurants on the square, Plaka is one of the most popular, but fish in general, and especially the prized red mullet (*barboúni*), is expensive.

The afternoon tourist traffic on **Sokrátous Street** should be pretty dense by now. Most of the things for sale are tacky odds and ends. Here you will also find (as in the new city) furriers touting their wares even in high summer. Despite its overall character, just before the street forks you will find one of

In the Old Town

the city's most beautiful cafés (*kafenía*), which is managed by a Turkish couple. Here the local men still drink traditional Greek coffee and play *távli,* Greek backgammon. The distinctive clatter of the tiles is one of the unforgettable sounds of summer on Rhodes.

After pausing for air and and a coffee, plunge back into the crowd and turn left into Ag Fanouriou. One of the medieval quarter's oldest and most famous thoroughfares, it is narrow, lit with wall lanterns and braced with flying arches to protect the houses during earthquakes. In a bid to reduce noise in the Old Town, it is officially pedestrianised by day, apart from residents' vehicles, delivery vans and taxis, but motorcycles still cause a problem, especially at night. Many taxi drivers refuse to go through the Old Town's more tortuous entrances, such as the Koskinou Gate, for fear of damaging their vehicles in the narrow lanes.

Leaving Ag. Fanourios, you come to **Platía Arínos** where you can sample the refurbished Turkish **Steam Baths of Mustafa Paşa**. Considered the finest in the East when they were built in 1558, the chambers are elaborately decorated and still heated by olive wood stoves. The huge dome-roofed main room with its ornamentation and marble floors is used only by men, while auxiliary rooms are reserved for women. Steam baths, masseurs (and masseuses) and an atmosphere of otherworldly calm make a visit to the baths an unusual experience. They are open from 7am–7pm daily except Sunday and Monday; bring your own soap and towels.

Located one block further on is the Nelly Dhimóglou open-air theatre (Andhronikou St, open May to October, performances Monday, Wednesday and Friday 9.20pm; for further information, tel: 2241 020157) where **folk dances** from all over Greece are presented. Nelly Dhimóglou, the leader of the dance troupe, has assiduously sought out, documented and choreographed traditional dances, previously handed down only through oral tradition.

Pavement cafés on Hippokrates Square

Continuing along **Ippodhamou**, on which several hostels are located, proceed to the rose-tinted **Mosque of Suleiman the Magnificent**, which looks along Sokrátous Street. This major landmark was built in 1522 to commemorate the sultan's victory over the knights and was rebuilt in 1808. Its superb, but unsafe, minaret had to be removed in 1989 and now the mighty edifice is crumbling and locked up. The **Islamic Library of Ahmet Havuz**, opposite, dates from 1793. It contains rare and valuable manuscripts including the chronicle of the siege of Rhodes from 1522, a collection of rare Arabic and Persian manuscripts and two priceless, illuminated 15th- and 16th-century Qur'ans.

Next on this itinerary is the **Palace of the Grand Masters** (8.30am–6pm; admission charge) on Platía Kleovoulou, which dominates both the old and new towns. There are several rooms open to the public and two permanent exhibitions, **Medieval Rhodes**, and **Rhodes 2,400 Years,** an archaeological exhibition. An excellent guide to the exhibitions with room plans and illustrations is on sale.

The Palace, which was inhabited during the Knights' period by the Grand Master and his guards, was badly damaged when the town fell to the Turks in 1522, then destroyed after an ammunition explosion in 1856. It was reconstructed by the Italians (1936) as a summer home for Mussolini and Victor Emmanuel III, neither of whom ever used it. Inside, a marble staircase leads up to interlinking rooms featuring marvellous mosaics taken from Kós. (You can join a tour around the walls of the Old Town every Tuesday and Saturday at 2.45pm, starting at the palace entrance.)

From the Palace we step out into the **Loggia of St John** where the Knights used to muster for action, originally linked to the Church of St John which was blown up when the arms cache was struck by lightning. Round off this tour by walking down the most famous street in the Knights' Quarter, **Odhós Ippotón** (the Street of the Knights), lined by the Inns of the various Tongues or nationalities, which were used as banqueting halls and lodgings for visitors, while the knights lived a monastic existence elsewhere. It's so well preserved you can almost hear the clatter of horseshoes on the cobbles.

Also here, and well worth visiting, is the **Archaeological Museum** (8.30am–3pm; admission charge), whose most famous item is a marble Aphrodite dating from the 1st century. On the corner of

Idyllic scene in the Old Town

the street a gift shop run by the Ministry of Culture sells replicas of statues and artefacts on show in the museum, all with certificates of authentication. North of here, on Platia Arghyrokástrou, is the **Museum of Decorative Arts** (Tues–Sun 8.30am–3pm), displaying costumes and crafts from across the Dodecanese, and the **Byzantine Museum** (Tues–Sun 8.30am–3pm), containing icons and frescoes.

A Stroll through the New City

A half-day tour: breakfast in the New Market; walk via Eleftherías Street to the Mosque of Murad Reis; Turkish Cemetery; a swim and/or a visit to the Aquarium; Amerikis Street towards the city walls; a detour through the park, and stopping for a Greek coffee on Dhimokritas Street.

The **Port of Rhodes** has been a reloading point for export goods for thousands of years. This will be our starting point for a walk through the new city. Before setting out on **Odhós Eleftherías**

Mandraki Harbour

(Freedom Street), flanked by neoclassical structures, you may want to have coffee or something more substantial in the **Néa Agorá**, or New Market, where people come from all over Rhodes and the neighbouring islands of Hálki and Symi to buy essentials. The circular market hall is a lively, colourful place and the hub of the New Town, with fresh fruit and vegetable stalls, butcher's shops and bakers rubbing shoulders with stores specialising in nuts, gifts and duty-free drink. The market is full of little cafés and stalls selling everything from fresh orange juice to *souvláki* and *gyro* with pitta-bread, the giant kebabs (*gyros*) of meat gently spit-roasting.

As you stroll through the market you have to run the gauntlet

View of the Néa Agorá (New Market)

of waiters trying to drum up trade for their restaurants. The vulnerable and hungry should choose with care: the pavement cafés overlooking the harbour are pleasant spots to watch the world go by, but tend to be pricey. The snack bars within the market are cheap and cheerful and used by the locals.

The fish market in the centre of all the bustle is in an elaborate domed building, elevated high above the action. The rest of the market is full of stalls selling costume jewellery, belts and T-shirts. Local shoppers use some of the little bars here as post restantes for parcels being sent to neighbouring islands and outlying villages.

In contrast to the new market, which has existed since the turn of the 20th century, **Odhós Eleftherías** (Freedom Street), down which we now set off, sprang up during a yet later period of Italian building activity. It runs straight as an arrow out to the port and illustrates the Fascist era's love of monumental buildings (the present-day Bank of Greece and the main Post Office, for example).

On the right, as you proceed, you will see the fortifications which run around **Mandhráki Harbour**, the furthest outpost of which – **St Nicholas's Fort** – was intended to withstand the onslaughts of the Ottoman Turks. According to legend, it was here that the

famous **Colossus of Rhodes** was raised, though the precise placing of the great feet has never been determined. The statue, erected in homage to the sun god, Helios, is alleged to have been some 34m (112ft) tall, but it fell to pieces during an earthquake only 65 years after its completion. For some seven centuries, the bronze wreckage is said to have lain before the walls of the city, until a Syrian Jew loaded it on to 900 camels and transported it to his home. (More sober scientific estimates have placed the number of camels at 90 at the most.) Nevertheless, the bronze giant was counted among the Seven Wonders of the World and has become, along with the windmills and the coy Rhodian deer, synonymous with Rhodes.

Perched on pillars, a bronze stag and doe guard the entrance to the harbour at the point where the Colossus may have stood. Deer are the symbols of the city as they rid the island of snakes in antiquity. For years a herd of deer lived in the moat of the Old Town but now a sanctuary has been set up for them in Rhodini Park.

If you proceed straight ahead, behind the neo-Venetian Prefecture, you will run right into the elegant minaret of the **Mosque of Murad Reis**, the admiral of Sultan Suleiman the Magnificent who was killed in battle in 1522. The mosque, built in his honour, fronts the **Turkish Cemetery** where Islamic VIPs lie beneath elaborate turban-shaped tombstones. The British writer Lawrence Durrell lived within the cemetery's precincts in the grounds of Villa Kleovoulos at the end of World War II. As the British press attaché, he had the thankless task of re-establishing Rhodes' press. His book, *Reflections on a Marine Venus,* contains a humorous description of these chaotic, postwar years, during which, for a brief time, the native population was subordinate to British officers.

A surprise awaits you when you step into the garden to the west of the Turkish Cemetery. Here stands the former luxury hotel, **Des Roses,** constructed by the Italians in 1928 but abandoned in the 1940s. Newly renovated it is now Rhodes casino, where you can flutter away your surplus euros or just enjoy a relaxing cocktail.

Those who have had enough of sightseeing might want to take this opportunity to head for **Elli beach** which begins behind **Platía Kountouriótou**. Alternatively you can head for the **Aquarium** (open from 9am–9pm), at the most northern tip of the city. Besides the corals, sea horses and scorpions, you'll also encounter stuffed curiosities such as a seven-legged calf.

The way back brings us down **Amerikis Street**, which leads directly into the Old Town. A visit to the park may be a welcome diversion. There is an attractive café on **Dhimokratia Street** under cedar and plane trees, which is popular among high school students. Surrounded by their loud discussion, you can enjoy some more local colour before plunging back into the Old Town.

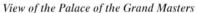

View of the Palace of the Grand Masters

A Full Day on the West Coast

Excursion from Rhodes City down the west coast road through Theologos, with its ruined Temple of Apollo, to Ancient Kamíros; Kritinía Castle; Kritinía, and its kafenía; fish dinner in Kámiros Skála (or wine tasting and dinner in Émbonas).

This car or motorcycle tour duplicates, for about a third of its route, the excursion outlined in Tour 4, 'Through Paradhíssi to the Valley of the Butterflies'. However, today we will not be turning off for Paradhíssi but will, instead, continue in the direction of Kamiros. The terrain on the west coast is not as wild, steep and fissured as the south of the island, but the climate is fresher and usually gets the full force of the Meltemi wind.

The first significant site, which you will pass after about 20km (12 miles), is the village of **Theologos**, also called Tholos, where the remains of an ancient **Temple of Apollo** are found. Among the artefacts on the site is a marble tablet listing the names of priests, eloquent testimony to the former importance of the cult.

Approximately 3km (2 miles) past Kalavardha, an avenue of pines on the left leads to the smallest settlement of the historic Dorian

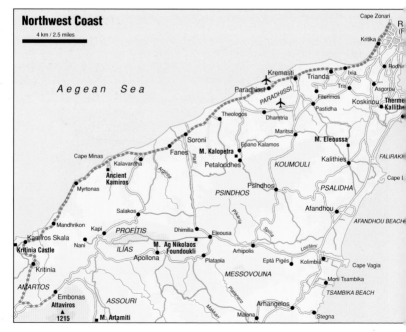

Remains at Kamiros

Three City League, **Ancient Kamíros** (open 8.30am–5pm, closed Monday). Kamíros, the flourishing but mysteriously abandoned Doric city discovered in 1859, is one of the west coast's major archaeological attractions. It was a thriving agricultural community during the 5th century BC and is now one of the best-preserved Classical Greek city sites.

The original ground-plan is exposed – you can even see the plumbing – along gently shelving terraces with stunning sea views west to Crete. Although named after the grandson of Helios, Kamíros was founded by Althaemenes of Crete and was probably destroyed in an earthquake in 142BC, although no-one is certain. The city lay forgotten for centuries until the British Consul Bilotti and French archaeologist Alzman began excavations where villagers had found ancient graves. The necropolis or cemetery yielded many 3rd-century BC treasures, several in the British Musuem and others, like the touching marble stele of Krito and her dead mother, in the Archaeological Museum in Rhodes Town.

The lay-out of the streets and houses is clearly defined, punctuated by the pillars of temples and topped by the remains of a great stoa. Sights include the remains of a 3rd-century BC Doric Temple, possibly of Pythian Apollo and altar to Helios; Hellenistic shops and houses, one with part of its colonnade reconstructed; public

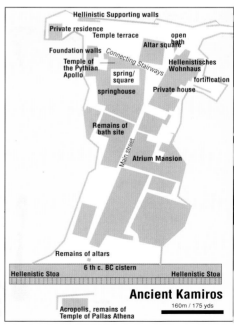

baths; and a giant 6th-century BC water cistern which could supply 400 families.

The remains of the 6th-century BC Temple of Athena Polias are on the top terrace, below which are vestiges of the once-magnificent Doric Stoa, 206m (640 ft) long. The area behind the stoa was the agora or market place, and to the left is a row of pits where treasures were stored. Unlike other sites on Rhodes, Kamíros was undisturbed by Byzantium, Christianity or the Knights. After a brief stop for refreshments at one of the tavernas on the coastal road below the site, head towards Kámiros Skála, the former port of Ancient Kamíros, with the ruins of **Kritinía Castle** perched on the crags above. Follow the signs to the castle, right up a gravel road through the farmland to the castle walls. Heavily fortified by the Knights of St John, the 15th-century ruins are perched above the sea with wonderful views to Hálki, the deserted island of Alimiá and on a fine day down to Kárpathos. Inland you can also see the whitewashed village of Kritinía, founded by Cretan settlers. While clambering over the castle ruins take care – there is a sheer drop from the battlements.

Back at the main road again, a few kilometres further uphill is the turn-off for the village of **Kritinía**. A detour off the main road is worthwhile for the small Folk Museum located on the outskirts of the village, and in the centre are two *kafenía* which have preserved their typical village character. These traditional Greek cafés are interesting for their attractive pink and turquoise colour schemes. Stroll through the village to see other traditional structures and architectural elements. Kritinía was founded by the son of a Cretan king. An oracle had prophesied that the son would kill his father and so the young man departed and founded the village of Kritinía on Rhodes. He lived there peacefully until his aged father, near death and desirous of seeing his son one last time, sailed over from Crete. Unfortunately, his fleet was thought to be hostile, and the oracle's portent came true.

Now there is a choice between two alternatives: free wine or great fish. **Émbonas**, the main wine-producing area of Rhodes and home of the Emery winery, offers wine tastings to visitors (further information on Émbonas is detailed in Tour 10). If fish appeals more than wine, head back to Kámiros Skála, the small fishing harbour and berth for ferries to Hálki. There are three good fish restaurants, all popular at weekends (Kalamares is an excellent choice, but the furthest place, Taverna Loukas, is a favourite lunchtime haunt and meeting place for anyone heading to Hálki). After an early meal, a dip in the wine-dark Aegean concludes your tour of the historical and gastronomic highlights of the west coast.

Through Paradhíssi to the Valley of the Butterflies

A half-day trip from Rhodes City, via Paradhíssi, to the Valley of the Butterflies (Petaloúdhes); Psinthos; Pastidha; Maritsa; the Filérimos Plateau and Monastery; Ialyssós; Tris, and its tavérna.

Set out on this tour as early as possible, because there is a lot to cover in half a day. Naturally, you can lengthen your stay at the suggested stops and extend this tour into a whole day. But whatever you decide, you should take along good hiking shoes and some provisions. One more thing: if you ride, you'll have an opportunity to do so at **Mike's Horses**, in the area of Mount Filérimos (tel: 94277, open from 9am–1pm, and 4–8pm.)

Your route first takes you out of Rhodes City in a westerly direction towards Paradhíssi airport, passing many hotels and commercial buildings that have sprung up along this route. Villages such as **Kremastí** (famous for its festival for the Dormition of the Virgin Mary in August with stalls and fun-fair) and **Triánda**, which were lively communities of the **Ialyssós** region several thousand years ago, are today continuously expanding strips of package tour accomoda-tion, their village centres oblit-erated by development.

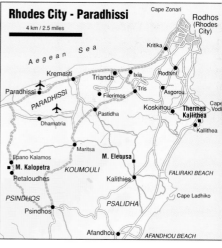

About 3km (2 miles) after Paradhíssi, turn left into the little road for **Kalamonas**. Proceed through the village and after about 2km (1 mile) you will arrive at the entrance to **Petaloúdhes**, the Valley of the Butterflies (which are really moths). The Jersey Tiger moths once gathered in their thousands from July to September, attracted by the scent of oriental amber and sweet gum trees, but now their numbers have dwindled. The moths are dull brown at rest, but their wings flash scarlet when they fly, so few people can resist the temptation to set them in motion. Now signs ban clapping and any other noise likely to disturb them.

Of course, even without the fauna, a hike here is well worth your time. The path guides you through a surprisingly green vale lined

*Restored monast.
buildings at Filerin*

with unusual trees and punctuated by springs, but the water is not safe to drink, or even wash fruit in. Flowing through the middle of the 2km (1 mile) long gorge, is a brook easily crossed by wooden bridges. If you want to rest after your hike, you will find a cosy *tavérna* at the end of the valley.

We continue now on a winding rural road through **Psinthos**, **Maritsa** and **Pastidha** in the direction of **Mount Filérimos**. Although not particularly attractive, Psinthos is historically important as the battle that was waged here on 17 May 1912 marked the end of the Turkish occupation.

A small detour takes you to a Byzantine chapel just outside Maritsa. Head left towards Kalaminas then about 300m (328yds) before the entrance to the village, and continue until you cross a bridge about 1km (half a mile) further on. Five hundred metres (547yds) to the left stands the late Byzantine church of **Ághios Nikólaos Foundouklís**, which gets its name from the hazelnut trees *(foundoukies)* that used to grow in the area.

A remarkable detail on the interior frescoes are the eyes of the saints, all of which have been stabbed out. The Turks were not, as is commonly thought, responsible for this desecration. Instead, it is a manifestation of medieval superstition. At that time eye disorders were 'treated' by taking mortar from the eyes of holy frescoes, beating it into a powder and then mixing it into an infusion drunk by the patient.

From **Maritsa** proceed straight on to the centre of **Pastidha**. Here a street sign points the way to Ialyssós. The asphalt, however, turns to gravel beyond the village. After a straight stretch of one or two kilometres, the road forks. The road to the right leads to the previously mentioned riding stables; the left fork goes up to the **Filérimos Plateau**, which lies 267m (876ft) above sea level. If you want to hike, tighten your laces at the first hairpin turn. Count on a good hour, longer in high summer. Because of the dense forest here, it is pleasantly cool in autumn and spring. The route now winds uphill through stands of fragrant pine and cypress. Lovely views of the Aegean Sea and beyond the City of Rhodes make the climb worthwhile.

Filérimos translates as 'Friend of Solitude'. Byzantine era hermits, who erected a **monastery** here in the early Middle Ages, gave this name to the mountain. At the top you will see the remains of an old basilica next to the large car-park. However, first take some time to inspect the **monastery** grounds. The monastery itself is famous for its Calvary or Stations of the Cross, an avenue with monuments depicting Christ's Crucifixion which leads to a towering Crucifix where you can climb the internal stairs and look out over the plain.

As is usual on Rhodes, layers of ruins lie beneath other ruins. Thus, the baptistry, which still exists in fragments next to the renovated bell tower, was erected on the site of an ancient temple. Ialyssós, formerly 'Ahaia', is supposed to have been settled two millennia before the arrival of the Ahaians. Here on the summit, next to the monastery church, was the **Temple of Athena Poliadhos and Zeus Polieas**.

Those interested in a detailed art historian's survey of the Filérimos Plateau can obtain a special guide book from the kiosk by the monastery church. Also available here is a famed seven-herb liqueur called *koleander*, which is brewed by Italian monks and is supposed to benefit the digestive system.

Proceed downhill again in the direction of **Triánda**. At the last hairpin curve on the mountain, a sign points towards **Tris**, situated off the main Trianda road away from all the tourist development. This settlement, not even indicated on many maps, has one of the island's best restaurants, **Ta Koupiá** (open for dinner only). Very popular with discerning Rhodians and an international clientele, it specialises in Greek cuisine, and is located on the main street.

Filerimos
20 m / 22 yds

Temple of Athena Poliados and Zeus Polieas

Cloisters

Gallery

Knights' Church

Belfry

Spring

Early Christian Baptistry

Abbot's Residence

IALYSSOS

Ialyssós, in antiquity one of the three administrative regions of the island alongside Líndhos and Kamíros, was essentially an agrarian community. There was no city of Ialyssós, *per se,* but only a loose linkage of communities which lay around the mountain. But the region, which in pre-Christian times administered the entire northern tip of the island, was unusually wealthy, as finds on the slopes of Filérimos have demonstrated.

The placement of Ialyssós' fortress – in an easterly direction from the monastery – was desirable from a strategic standpoint. From the peak, the entire northern end of the island can be surveyed. Whoever wished to conquer Rhodes had to concentrate their forces on Ialyssós and Mount Filérimos before they had any chance of conquering the rest of the island.

The Kallithéas Hot Springs and Monte Smith

A half-day tour from Rhodes City to Thérme Kallithéas, a Moorish baths complex; the lively resort of Faliráki; a climb up to the ancient Acropolis on Monte Smith; the day ends with a first-rate dinner at Vlahos Tavérna.

This afternoon excursion south to **Faliráki** takes you out of town through urban landscapes dotted with industrial installations, docks, and repair shops and intersected by rather dull streets. The view remains the same beyond the city limits. Building cranes, excavated plots and half-finished hotel bunkers all amply illustrate how every metre of the northeastern coast is being exploited for the purposes of tourism.

After about 9km (6 miles), you will see a sign for the **Hot Springs of Kallithéas**. This picturesque spa with its Arab arches and domes was built by the Italians at the beginning of the 20th century. To be sure, the mineral springs of Kallithéas were already known in ancient times. The physician Hippokrates, who was born in 460BC on the island of Kós, extolled their beneficial effects on liver, kidney and rheumatic complaints.

Popular as a film and TV set, the spa has otherwise been disused since the end of World War II and as a consequence has a rather surreal feel with its crumbling facades. However, with a little imagination, one can resurrect the elegant international coterie in the mosque-like hall who came to 'take the waters'. The park alone,

The Hot Springs at Kallithéas

Thérme Kallithéas, built by the Italians in an Arab style

with its waving palms, pruned hedges, columns, and its continuously changing view of the Aegean, makes a longer expedition worthwhile. After viewing the buildings, take a dip in the sea at the little swimming cove below the springs.

Try to avoid the standard, rather dull fare on offer in most of the restaurants in **Faliráki**, which is 4km (2 miles) further south. This village, built solely for tourists, has some 200,000 beds available, including many belonging to holiday clubs for young adults. It has good nightlife, some of the island's finest beaches, and is connected to Rhodes by a regular bus service. From the gigantic water slide to the tennis courts, saunas, surfing and go-kart racing facilities, you can work out in style. You can bungee jump, and there's an extensive mall.

The return route leads back via the same road to the edge of Rhodes City. At the Supermarket Miko, located to the right just behind the city boundary sign, self-catering holiday-makers may want to stock up on reasonably priced goods from other parts of Europe, from Irish butter to Italian salami and German coffee. Particularly worth noting are reasonably priced Greek wines and international spirits. The supermarket's opening hours are posted at the entrance.

To reach your last stop, the ancient ruins atop **Monte Smith**, turn left behind the small bridge at the cemetery and drive straight on down Ana Marías Street, on the other side of the main road to Líndhos. At the end of this street, turn right into Themistokli Sofouli Street until you reach Dhiagoridhon, which branches to the left, leading you directly to the old stadium. However, be attentive. The direction of this one-way street changes frequently, and it is quite probable you will reach your goal after several detours.

If you park your car at the corner of Dhiagoridhon and Themistokli Sofouli streets, you can combine your expedition through the ancient City of Rhodes with a half-hour-long hike up to the hill of Monte Smith. The hill's real name is Ághios Stéfanos, but this alternative name marks it as the heights from which British Admiral Sir Sidney Smith kept watch for the Napoleonic Fleet. Even if you're not that interested in British military history, it's well worth the trip for the wonderful twilight panorama over Rhodes town to the Turkish coast.

As in many other places on Rhodes, Italian archaeological groups have tried their hand at restoring the ancient remains on Monte Smith. As a result, the complete reconstruction of the **stadium**, 200m (219yds) wide and 530m (580yds) long, as well as the small **amphitheatre**, with its marble staircases, provides a vivid picture of the ancient Rhodian lifestyle. On the other hand, it takes a stretch of the imagination to conjure up an image of the glory that was once Rhodes City from the four remaining columns of the **Temple of Apollo** or the wreckage of the Acropolis.

Then, if you are too tired to face the descent on foot, catch the bus No 5 which plies, every 30mins, backwards and forwards between the Temple of Apollo and Mandhráki. It will deposit you back where you started at the beginning of this itinerary. You can conclude your excursion with a first-rate Greek meal at the excellent **Mystagogia** restaurant in the old town.

Accommodation

Hotels in Rhodes are graded in six categories – luxury and "A" to "E". There are hotels in all categories up to A-Class in most resorts, and luxury hotels in Rhodes Town, Ixiá, Faliráki and Kálathos, Rates vary between off-season, shoulder season and high season (July and August). In off and shoulder seasons hotel owners may offer further discounts (up to 50 percent) depending on demand.

LUXURY

Hilton Rhodes Resort, Ixiá, tel: 2241 075 000, fax: 2241 076 690, www.rhodes.hilton.com. Classic Hilton hotel with plush interior. Very handy for the airport and close to the beach. Indoor and outdoor pool.

Rodos Palace, Ixiá, tel: 2241 025222, fax: 2241 025350, www.rodos.palace.gr. Grand old-world elegance.

Mediterranean, Ko 35–37, tel: 2241 024662, fax: 2241 022828, www.mediterranean.gr. An older hotel next to the beach in the New Town. Excellent service and large rooms decorated in washed earth colours.

Miramare Wonderland, Ixiá, tel: 2241 096251, fax: 2241 095954, www.mamhotel.gr. Right on the beach and ideal for holidays and relaxation. Comprises bungalow suites.

Paradise Royal Mare, Kallithea, tel 2241 066060, fax 2241 066066, www.aldemarhotels.com. Large complex on east side of Rhodes. Sea or garden view. Pool with large waterslide for kids.

Rodian Amathus Beach Hotel, Ixiá, tel: 2241 089900, fax: 2241 089 901, www.rodian-beach.gr. Large Cypriot-owned complex. Two pools, one with rapids.

Rodos Park Suites, Riga Fereou 12, tel: 2241 024613, fax: 2241 024613, www.rodospark.gr. Luxury 'apartment hotel' in the middle of the city park and overlooking the Old City walls.

"A" CLASS

Athineon, Vyronos 17, tel: 2241 026112, fax 2241 026459. Standard hotel near the city walls. Bright and pleasant rooms with kitchenette.

Dionysus, Ippoton, Ixiá, tel: 2241 023021, fax: 2241 034401, www.dionysos-hotel.gr. Attractively renovated, with beautiful garden, pool and restaurant.

Ibiscus, Nisyrou 17, tel: 2241 024 421, fax: 2241 027 283, e-mail: ibiscus@rhotel.gr. Pleasant and friendly hotel near the casino. Marble and wood decor, slightly old-fashioned.

Mansion Marco Polo, Agiou Fanouriou 42, tel: 2241 025 562, fax: 2241 025 562, www.marcolopolomansion.web.com. Classy pension in traditional Ottoman caravanserai. Has featured in many glossy magazines.

"B" CLASS

Electra Palace, Paralia Ialysou, tel: 2241 092521, fax: 2241 092 038, e-mail: elecrho@otenet.gr. Classic resort-style hotel close to the beach.

Hotel Cava d'Oro, Kistiniou 15, tel: 2241 036980, fax: 2241 077332. Cosy pension against the walls of the Old Town. The British actor Michael Palin stayed here when making the TV programme *Pole to Pole*.

Le Petit Palais, Griva 3, tel: 2241 022781, fax: 2241 021411, www.mitsishotels.com. New Town centre hotel with large, airy rooms.

Pension Andreas, Omirou 28D, Old Town, tel: 2241 034156, fax: 2241 074285, www.hotelandreas.com. Rustic pension with pleasant rooms in quiet part of Old Town. Superb views from breakfast room.

SELECTED INEXPENSIVE HOTELS

Casa Antica, Amarandou 8, New Town, tel: 2241 026206, fax: 2241 077 662. Simple hostelry, with pleasant high-ceilinged rooms. Lush courtyard.

Hotel Anastasia, 28th Oktovriou 46, New Town, tel: 2241 028007, fax: 2241 021815, www.anastasia-hotel.com. Old-style hotel with clean rooms. Pleasant garden with banana trees and resident tortoises.

Hotel Spot, Perikleous 21, Old Town tel: 2241 034 737, fax: 2241 034737, www.rodosisland.gr. Spruce budget hotel close to the Old Town action. Cosy decor.

New Village Inn Konstantopedos 10, New Town, tel: 2241 034937, fax: 2241 034937, e-mail: newvillageinn@rho.forthnet.gr. Small and cosy hostelry with a leafy courtyard. Comfortable beds.

Pension Olympos, Agiou Fanouriou 56, Old Town, tel: 2241 033567, fax 2241 033567. Family-run establishment on one of the Old Town's prettiest streets.

Car & Bike Hire

Alamo/National, 28th Oktovriou 18, tel: 2241 073570.

Drive, Afstralias 2, tel: 2241 035141.

Kosmos, Papalouka 31, tel: 2241 074374.

Orion, Georgiou Leondos 36, tel: 2241 022137.

Rent a Harley, 28th Oktovriou 80, tel: 2241 074925, www.astronet.gr/rentaharley.

Restaurants

GREEK SPECIALITIES AND FISH RESTAURANTS

Alexis, Sokratous 8, Old Town, tel: 2241 029347. Classy fish taverna with extensive wine list.

Begleri, Klavdiou Pepper 105–7, Zefyros Beach, tel: 2241 033 353. Attractive *ouzeri* and fish taverna on southern side of the New Town.

Dinoris, Museum Square, Old Town, 2241 025824. Fish restaurant in 14th-century building. Excellent fish dishes and salads.

Fotis Melathron, Parodos Sokratous 41, Old Town, tel: 2241 023272. Very impressive location and ambience. Classic Greek cuisine.

Fotis, Menekleous 8, Old Town, tel: 2241 027 359. Unpretentious fish taverna known for its high quality.

Giannis Restaurant, Koskinou Village, tel 2241 063547. Superb village atmosphere on back streets. Top-class Greek grills and *mezedes*.

Masasoura, Maritsa Village, tel: 2241 048109. Good steak and grill house in rural Rhodes. Good for Sunday lunch.

Metaxy Mas, Klavdiou Pepper 116, New Town, tel: 2241 073456. Excellent, low-key *ouzeri* by the beach, serving a mainly Greek clientele.

Myrovolos, Lahitos 13, Old Town, 2241 038693. Un-touristy *ouzeri*-style hole in the wall. Often has live music.

Mystagogia, Themistokleous 5, Old Town, tel: 2241 032981. Greek eatery in secluded corner. Excellent *mezedes*.

Nireas, Sofokleous 22, Old Town, tel: 2241 021703. Classy fish restaurant.

Palia Istoria, Mitropoleos & Dendrinou, New Town, tel: 2241 032421. Greek-international cuisine with fine wines.

Pigi Fasouli Estatorio, Psinthos Village, tel: 2241 050071. Well-known rural taverna in idyllic setting. Rhodian specialities.

To Steki Tou Tsima, Peloponisou 22, New Town, tel: 2241 074390. Old-style no-nonsense fish taverna with imaginative fish *mezedes*.

ASIAN AND INTERNATIONAL RESTAURANTS

Dutch Inn, Iraklidon 5, Ixiá, tel: 2241 092901. Authentic Dutch cuisine with added Dutch-Indonesian specials.

Gulliver, Miramare Wonderland Hotel, tel: 2241 096251. Greek-international cuisine with some excellent salads.

Indian Star, Alexandrou Diakou 24, New Town, tel: 2241 075100. Classic north Indian cooking in atmospheric location.

Kasbah, Platonos 4–8, Old Town, 2241 078633. Moroccan dishes with an emphasis on couscous specials.

L'auberge Bistrot, Praxitelous 21, Old Town, tel: 2241 034292. French nouvelle cuisine with Mediterranean overlays.

Locos, Iraklidon 76, Ialysos Village, tel: 2241 096680. Classic Mexican diner. Authentic decor.

Pagoda, Faliraki, tel: 2241 066 387. Chinese specialities with Thai influence.

Queen's Garden, Valaoritou 1, tel: 2241 035 360. Szechuan cooking.

Restaurant Rhobel, Georgiou Leondos 13-15, New Town, 2241 075938. Belgian cuisine fused with Greek ingredients.

Thavma en Kairo, Eleftheriou Venizelou 16–18, tel: 2241 025569. Multinational cuisine, in particular incorporating Greek, Asian and Scandinavian influences.

BRITISH CUISINE

Angelos, Polydorou & Agisandrou 34, tel: 2241 074185. A café/bar with breakfast, fish 'n' chips, scampi or steak and kidney pie on offer.

Molly's British Diner, Ferenikis 4, Trianda Village, tel: 2241 096477. Full English breakfasts plus roast beef and Yorkshire pudding.

Partners Bistro, Faliraki, tel 2241 085 620. Best of traditional British food in huge portions.

ITALIAN CUISINE

Capo el Metro, corner Mandilara & Griva, tel: 2241 024677. Fresh pasta, salads and hot baguettes.

La Casa di Pasta, Mandilara 28, tel: 2241 075 834. Excellent pasta.

HAUTE CUISINE

Marco Polo, Hilton Rhodes Resort, Ixiá, tel: 2241 075000. Eurasian fusion cuisine from a top German chef.

La Rotisserie, Rodos Palace Hotel, Ixiá, tel: 2241 025 222. Old-style French gourmet cuisine.

Ta Kioupia, Argonafton 12, Ialysos, tel: 2241 093 448. Enormous spread of Greek gourmet, set-menu dishes. Extensive wine list.

Nightlife

OLD TOWN

The Old Town is for shopping, relaxing romantic meals and leisurely strolls. There is a clutch of classy cafeterias around Sofokleous – Café Street – that are popular for coffee, spirits and gossip.

Café Basara, Sofokleous 11–12. An Australian-owned bar right in the thick of Café Street. A good see and be-seen hangout.

Mango Café Bar, Dorieos 3. Boasting cheap drinks and smooth schmoozing. Popular with the diving fraternity. Internet access too.

Mousiko Café, Platonos 3. Popular hangout for hip young Greeks. Good for people-watching.

Rahati, Sofokleous 1. An Ottoman-style café with scatter cushions and rugs. Smoke a *nargiles* (hookah) pipe here if you like.

Resalto Club, Plateia Damagitou. Greek bouzouki club. Open after 11pm Fri and Sat. Patronised mainly by Greeks, but all are welcome.

Stavros Bar, Ippodamou 32. British-style bar on a narrow, pebbled street. Draught English beer and snacks.

NEW TOWN

After dark, most foreign visitors gravitate to the New Town where there are raucous bars, multi-bar clubs and discos. Bar Street (Orfanidou) is where most of the fast-packed action is.

Baroque, Alex Diakou 19. Housed in a restored classical mansion. Good for coffees and cocktails and keeping cool on hot, sultry nights.

Colorado Entertainment Centre, Akti Miaouli & Orfanidou 57. Enormous club with three buzzing bars and non-stop action.

Nick's Cardinal Sports Bar, 28th Oktovriou 52. Chilled out homely bar with regular sports broadcasts from Sky Sports.

O'Reillys, Apolloniou 61. Lots of drinking and singing and Guinness and Kilkenny on tap

Rock Idols, Orfanidou 29. A mix of hard rock and mellow mood music permeates this popular bar.

Sticky fingers, Anthoula Zervou 6. Live rock features several nights a week at this long-standing favourite rave haven.

Swing, Orfanidou 54. Big on glitter and mirror balls, Swing is the disco spot in town, with soul, R 'n' B plus other disco classics.

Sound & Light

Get an impressive introduction to the history of Rhodes at this ever-popular sound and light show in Rhodes' Municipal Gardens. English-language presentations take place at 9.15pm on Monday, Wednesday and Friday and at 11.15pm on Tuesday, Thursday and Saturday. The show starts on hour earlier from 1 September to 31 October.

ARCHANGELOS

With its 3,300 residents, the town of **Arhángelos** (Archangelos) is the second largest settlement on the island, located on the east coast 29km (18 miles) south of Rhodes Town. In spite of its inland location, it attracts a large, mostly German package-tour market and is thus well-endowed with tavernas, banks, nightclubs, souvenir shops etc. The name of the town refers to the Archangel Michael, to whom the main town church is dedicated. Arhángelos is proud of its ceramic industry and carpet 'factory', where you can order a carpet woven according to your own specifications, as well as *kereloúdhes* (rag rugs). The leather industry also used to be important, and traditional knee-high boots – originally worn to protect legs from snakes in the fields – can be made to measure by local cobblers, but they don't come cheap. Made from sturdy cowhide and goatskin (snakes hate the smell of goats) the colourful boots can be worn on either foot.

Located above the village are the ruins of a **Crusader fortress**, constructed by Grand Master Orsini in 1467 to provide protection against the Turks.

There are a number of beaches that can be reached by car or motorbike. **Stegna** is the closest at 3km (2 miles) away; a better option, however is **Agáthi**, reached via the little resort and fishing port of Haráki, which is overlooked by the crumbling Knights' castle of Feraklós. Attractions around Arhangelos include Tsambíka Monastery, on a volcanic headland behind Kolimbia, and a place of pilgrimage for women hoping to conceive a child.

Arhángelos and Environs

A full-day tour starting in Arhángelos, where you can visit the potter Panaghiotis; then proceed to the Seven Springs (Eptá Pighés); and Kolimbia Beach for a swim and dinner; followed by an afternoon hike up to Tsambíka Monastery.

It's not necessary to set out on this tour at the crack of dawn, since there are no great distances to cover. Have a big breakfast

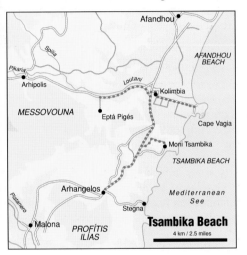

at one of the many breakfast bars on the main street in **Arhángelos** and then take a quick look at the colourful woven rugs flapping in the breeze outside shops surrounding the bus stop. Folded, these carpets will fit into any suitcase and, at approximately €15–20, are reasonably priced souvenirs.

Continue to the centre of the village, where the two main roads meet, and follow the signs by the bridge to **Stegna**. This road through the fields leads you to the top of a hill which has a fine view

towards the sea. Here, turn left and, after roughly 500m/yds), you will reach the cottage of the potter Panaghiotis, whose kiln can be spotted just to the right on the edge of the path. As you enter his shady yard, you'll probably find him sitting before his potter's wheel. Although he doesn't know you, he will almost certainly greet you as though you were an old friend and offer you an *oúzo* to sip as you examine his assortment of ceramics, including amphoras, carfted according to ancient traditions. Panaghiotis also accepts commissions. You may like to take a look at Panaghiotis's unique wooden bed, intended for alfresco afternoon siestas and positioned at the edge of the cliff above the sea.

After visiting the potter, follow the road back through the fields and turn right into the main road to Rhodes Town, which leads steeply uphill. From here you can enjoy a good view of **Tsambíka Bay** and, perched high above, Tsambíka Monastery. Then proceeding down, take the left fork in the road in the direction of **Eptá Pighés/Arhipolis**. After 3km (2 miles), take a sharp left turn in the middle of a right-hand curve and head uphill to **Seven Springs**

Inviting sea and sand: Kolimbia Beach

(Eptá Pighés), one of the island's lushest beauty spots nestling in the pinewoods. There's a car park and restaurant beneath the shady trees. A stream flows just below the restaurant, part of the irrigation system installed by the Italians to water the orange grove of **Kolimbia**. It is fed by the same seven springs which gave the place its name.

The entrance to a tunnel is located just a metre or so from the restaurant and, at the end of the tunnel, the stream ends in a light green pool. Those not afraid to roll up their trousers and wade into the dark will be richly rewarded by what they find on the other side. If you don't fancy this, you can reach the place more easily by simply climbing the hill. In addition to the pool, you may want to photograph the colourful peacocks which live in the restaurant grounds.

After a rest and a cool drink in the shade, return to Kolimbia crossroads. Head over the main road down an arrow-straight avenue of eucalyptus trees in the direction of **Kolimbia Beach**. Here, it's up to you which way to turn when the road forks. In recent years, this whole area has become a prime destination for sun-seeking foreign tourists, and a series of new hotels and restaurants have sprung up to serve their needs. On Kolimbia's beautiful

beach, you will find loungers and umbrellas as well as facilities for water sports and boating excursions.

Leaving Kolimbia Beach, return to the main road, where after about 2km (1 mile) a turn left leads to **Tsambíka Monastery**. Avid hikers should park their cars beyond the first hairpin turn. Others will want to creep a bit further up the mountain in first gear. The steep track ends at a long flight of steps rising through the pinewoods to the monastery, which is perched on the conical mountain peak. The monastery's chapel has long been a place of pilgrimage to childless women, who come to pray to the miraculous icon of the Virgin Mary for help in conceiving. The 11th-century icon was found on the mountain by a childless couple, and the wife, believed to be barren, later conceived. If the pilgrims' prayers for motherhood are answered they pledge to name their children Tsambíkos or Tsambíka in gratitude – names that are unique to Rhodes.

The splendid view from the summit, at 300m (984ft), takes in Faliráki to the northeast, Cape Líndhos to the southwest and, to the west, the imposing Atávyros Massif.

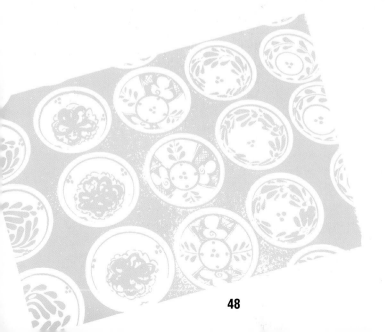

An afternoon tour from Arhángelos, via the old national road, to Malona and Haráki; then, a 1½ hour walk to Feraklós Castle. The day ends with a fish dinner at the Argo Restaurant.

Leaving Arhángelos at around 3 or 4pm, and wearing good walking shoes, drive south, following signs for the Old National Road posted

Haráki's beach promenade and the fortress of Feraklós

at the intersection on the main street. After 6km (4 miles) you will reach **Malóna,** and the so-called fruit basket of Rhodes. This fertile valley is the site of Rhodes' largest orange grove. The oranges, which are harvested twice a year (end of May and end of October), are outstanding as juice oranges, so purchase a kilo of *portokália* in Malóna.

Another gourmet attraction in Malóna is the village bakery. Here you will find the most delicious bread on Rhodes, baked in traditional wood-fired ovens. The fragrant sourdough loaves may be bought hot from the oven on weekday afternoons. For those new to the area, the bakery, used mainly by local people, may be a little difficult to find – Malóna, and the neighbouring village of Massari, are still wholly intact Greek villages which have not succumbed to the tourism rampant at the beach settlement of Haráki.

49

Fish tavérna in Haráki

To avoid getting lost, stop just before you reach the little bridge on the village road, and ask a passerby for directions to the bakery: *Pou íne o foúrnos?*

Now double-back to the traffic lights at the entrance to the village where, a couple of metres to the right, you reach the main road for Líndhos/Rhodes Town. Beyond the intersection, the road leads straight ahead to **Haráki**, whose special charm lies in the graceful, Italian promenade stretching all the way around the port. Here you will find – a rarity on Rhodes – many Greek tourists, who have high expectations indeed when it comes to Greek food and drink.

However, before you settle down for a meal, make the 45-minute ascent to the **Fortress of Feraklós**, a 14th-century Crusader castle enthroned on the hill above Haráki. To reach the ruins, climb up the steps on the southwest side of the hill. Looking out from the citadel, you will have a superb view over the coast north of Haráki.

At the end of the beach promenade at Haráki is the fish restaurant **Argo**, where you can make your own selection from the morning's catch. Among the seafood on offer, red mullet *(barboúnia),* whitebait *(marídhes)* and prawns *(garídhes)* are all excellent options. Don't forget that the prices quoted on the menu are by weight and not per portion.

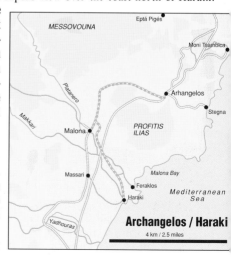

Accommodation

HOTEL KATERINA
Tel: 2244 022861
45 rooms, restaurant, swimming pool. Around 15 minutes from the centre, overlooking Arhángelos.

HOTEL ANAGROS
Tel: 2244 022248
26 rooms. Around 10 minutes from the centre, panoramic view of the town.

HOTEL ARHANGELOS
Tel: 2244 022230
18 rooms. Situated near the centre.

HOTEL DIMITRA
Tel: 2244 022668
Family-owned hotel.

PENSION NIKOS
Tel: 2244 022815
11 clean, simple rooms plus five studios which are ideal for families. Air-conditioning. Five minutes from the centre.

PENSION TARALLIS
Ten minutes from the centre.

Restaurants

RESTAURANT SAVVAS
Tel: 2244 023125
Greek specialites. Large terrace. Situated on the main street.

TAVERNA AFENTIKO
On the main street.

RESTAURANT KANARIS
Just off the main street.

TAVERNA HELLAS
On the central square.

Vehicle Rental

RENT A CAR ANTONIO
Tel: (2244) 022524

RENT A CAR TSAMPIA
Tel: (2244) 022145

Tourist Information

TSAMPIKA TRAVEL
Tel: (2244) 022145

Ancient Lindos

Along with Kamíros and Ialyssós, Lindos (Líndhos) was one of Rhodes' three ancient settlements. This once thriving city, whose golden age began with the arrival of the Dorians, sustained itself primarily through seafaring and trade. It prospered due to its favourable, sheltered location on the island's east coast. As a member of the League of Six Cities or the Doric Hexapolis, it administered the entire southeastern segment of the island. By as early as the 7th century AD, it had a population of 16,000. The city cultivated overseas trade relationships and minted its own coins as well as maintaining such colonies as Sicily, Spain and the Balearics.

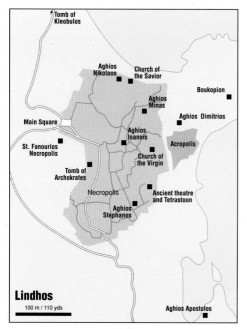

The pioneering Lindhian maritime law was accepted as binding for sea travel in general. Under the 'tyrant' Kleovoulos, one of the seven sages of the ancient world, it developed into a cultural centre of international renown. Two marble tablets, found on the Acropolis, record the roster of ancient VIPs: Herakles, Agamemnon and Helen of Troy, the King of Persia and Alexander the Great.

However, following the Persian Wars, its membership in the Delian League and, not least, with the rapid ascendancy of Rhodes City (founded in 408BC), the metropolis declined in significance. Lindhos did not regain its position as an important trading port until the invasion of the Venetians in around AD1200.

The Lindian Acropolis

Lindos Today

Nowadays, Lindos is a comparatively small village which bursts with visitors during the summer months. Half a million tourists a year stream through its narrow alleys. It is the island's main attraction, and its historical monuments have been placed under protection as a result. You have to park and walk into the village as traffic is banned.

The golden sands of Lindos Bay are packed and there are all kinds of watersports. By day the village hums with activity in the souvenir shops, bars and fast food places, from burger joints to *crêperies*, and after sun-down there's plenty of night life. There's a night club and disco with a swimming pool, and many of the old sea captains' mansions have been turned into trendy bars.

Accommodation is expensive and scarce. Although there are luxury hotels on the outskirts and a few pensions in the centre of the village, most Lindian houses have been taken over by British companies for self-catering holidays. Information about accommodation is available from the Tourist Police, whose office is in the main square.

Historical Tour of Lindos

Morning tour: an early breakfast at Alexis; ascent, by foot or donkey, to the Lindian Acropolis, with its ancient temple complex and medieval ramparts; a swim, with or without bathing suit, in the Aegean; a stroll by the 'Captains' Houses' of Lindos, followed by a visit to the Panaghía Church.

In order to escape the hordes who descend on Lindos during high season, you should wake as early as possible – 8am, at the latest – and head for the **Acropolis**. By setting out early, you will make the rather strenuous ascent in the cool of the morning, and avoid the long queues at the entrance to the site.

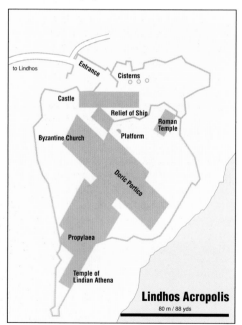

to Lindhos
Entrance
Cisterns
Castle
Relief of Ship
Roman Temple
Byzantine Church
Platform
Doric Portico
Propylaea
Temple of Lindian Athena

Lindhos Acropolis
80 m / 88 yds

Today, modern Lindos is a small town, which managed to retain its village character through the 1960s only to succumb to the influence of tourism in the 1970s. It's not too difficult to find your way round from the central bus stop but otherwise the maze of lanes can be confusing. Follow the main street down to the Church of the Panaghía, where the Acropolis is clearly signposted. You might want to grab a quick breakfast at **Alexis** on the way. If you don't want to walk up to the Acropolis you can take a donkey from behind the main square where the drivers wait with their donkey trains. Your 'donkey taxi' will take you around the northern inlet where you can admire the imposing citadel complex from below.

Pedestrians should take the steep steps which lead up from the village centre through the narrow alleys lined with gift shops, passing the pretty white houses with their picturesque courtyards. On the edge of the village, the main street becomes a dirt path,

Lindos' medieval ramparts

with steps cut from the stone of the Acropolis itself. Be very careful here. The steps are extremely slippery, worn smooth by the tramp of countless feet over the centuries. Lacemaking is a local craft and you might want to pause under the cedar trees, where tablecloths are offered for sale by Lindian women.

After inspecting these wares, you will find yourself at the entrance to the **Acropolis**. Purportedly, the site was first occupied by tribes which emigrated here from Asia Minor. They are believed to have first worshipped their mother-deity, **Líndhia**, a goddess imported from the East, in a grotto beneath the ancient temple site. Lindian myths later merged with the cult of the goddess **Athena**. The temple erected on the summit in honour of the Greek warrior-goddess is supposed to have been in existence at the time of the Ahaians and Dorians. Since then, it has been extensively remodelled, expanded and altered to fit the needs of subsequent generations of inhabitants. What you

see today above modern Lindos are the remains of buildings which were reconstructed after a huge fire in the temple in 320BC, as well as a medieval castle which was later integrated into the ancient site. As you enter the site, you will understand why the **Grand Masters** built upon the remains of the pre-Christian sanctuary. This site is a natural strategic stronghold, commanding views of both the interior of the island and of the coast.

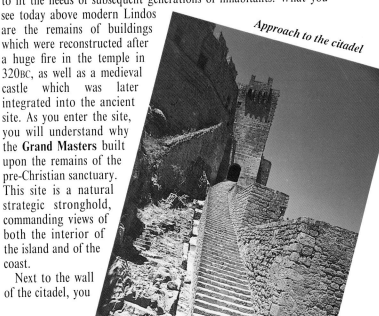

Approach to the citadel

Next to the wall of the citadel, you

Lush vegetation in the environs of Lindos

can still find the remains of **ancient cisterns** which supplied water to the residents. To the left, in front of the exterior stairs, the right-angled steps of which are part of the Italian renovation, you will find the 5th-century bas relief of an ancient trireme (galley developed as a warship) carved into the rock. The prow of the ship once held a statue of Aghisandher, priest of Poseidon, who, the inscription tells, was awarded a golden laurel wreath by the Lindhians for judging their athletic events.

The magnificence of this site, with its seamless marriage of architectural styles from several epochs, is clearly evident as you emerge from the defensive walls surrounding the medieval command post into the bright, open terrace laid out by the ancients. This was once the location of the **Stoa**, a hall bordered by tall columns, 20 of which have been reconstructed. Unfortunately, much of the site is covered in scaffolding. Among the niches, Doric columns and remains of medieval walls, you will see openings into the ancient system of cisterns before climbing to the upper terrace. Here is where the **Propylaea**, a colonnaded forecourt outside the **sanctuary to Lindian Athena**, was located. The temple at the top of the plateau, encompassed an area about 23m (75 ft) long and 8m (26 ft) wide. It housed the statue of the goddess, whose official status as patroness of the city of Lindos has been documented as dating from around the 4th century BC. The remains of the Temple of Lindian Athena are perched on the edge of the cliff and from this high vantage point, you have a goddess's-eye-view: to the left, below the Acropoli, is the **Bay of Lindos** with its beaches and, to the south, the **Bay of St Paul**, where the apostle is thought to have sheltered from a storm in AD51.

Take the donkey path down from the Acropolis for a dip in the Aegean at **Pallas Beach** directly below. The nudist beach is a few hundred metres beyond the sands.

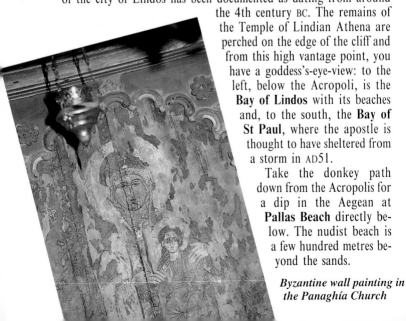

Byzantine wall painting in the Panaghía Church

After a dip, it's back to bustling little Lindos town. The tour coaches, which arrive every half hour, will have off-loaded an enormous number of visitors since you set out this morning. This uninterrupted stream makes the main street resemble a pedestrian mall back home. Despite the throng, it's worth stopping to take a closer look at the old houses. Beyond the huge stone walls you'll find the lovely Lindian *arhóndhika,* or sea captains' mansions, dating from the 15th to 18th centuries. Hidden away behind imposing doorways with embellished stone porticos in all kinds of styles, the houses are built around courtyards full of flowers, decorated with traditional black and white pebble mosaics, or *hoklákia.* Inside, the floors are also studded with pebbles in ancient patterns. The facades of the captains' houses are carved with Byzantine and eastern designs as well as twisted ropes and chains to symbolise the seafaring heritage of the owners. There are balconies built out over the alleyways as well as special captains' rooms over the doorways which guaranteed views of enemy movements out at sea.

Snow white Lindos

To round off your tour of Lindos, it's worth visiting the little **Panaghía Church**, which is in the centre of the village. This late Byzantine church of the Assumption of the Virgin Mary, or Panaghía, was built on the site of a 10th-century basilica and restored by Grand Master Pierre d'Aubuisson between 1489–90. The interior walls are almost covered in frescoes painted by Gregory of Symi in 1779 and refurbished in 1927. Look out for the painting of St Christopher depicted with the head of a jackal after he prayed to God to make him less attractive to women. Also particularly worthy of note here are the beautifully laid floors of pebble mosaic, which are so characteristic of the interior courtyards and living areas of the rich Lindians.

Rather than eat in the centre of the village – where a blatantly touristy scene prevails – you might like to stop at one of the restaurants on the road to Kalathos. **Panorama**, 3km (2 miles) out of town, serves prawns wrapped in bacon on skewers, and other delicacies. The restaurant has a lovely site, overlooking Vliha Bay and Lindos Bay Hotel.

The Tomb of the Tyrant and Evening in Lindos

An afternoon walk to the tomb of Kleovoulos; dinner at the Xenomania Restaurant; a visit to the Qupi bar; and late-night dancing
at the Acropolis or Epos discos. Begin in the late afternoon,
ideally about two hours before sunset so you will be sitting down
to dinner just as the sun begins its slow summer descent.

From the main square in Lindos, walk down Kleovoulos Street towards the beach, then follow the sign right to the restaurant Xenomania, and attractive open-air restaurant and bar. The route leads
through a small olive grove. Behind the restaurant, the path leads
out onto a spit of land. Continue straight on, towards the windmill
before the **Hill of Kleovoulos**.

Clamber uphill and soon you'll find yourself standing before an
impressive monument, originally covered by a half-dome roof. According to tradition, this building – which dates from the 1st
century BC – is the **Tomb of Kleovoulos**. As 'tyrant', Kleovoulos
ruled Lindos for 40 years during the 6th century BC. His tomb –
if it is his tomb – was erected several centuries after his death. Considered one of the seven wise men of ancient Greece, Kleovoulos
has gone down in history not only as a notable ruler, but also as
a poet and philosopher and the source of the well-known saying:
'Moderation in all things' ('*pan, metron, ariston*' in Greek).

From here, you will have a wonderful view of the Bay of Lindos,
the white houses of the village and, towering above, the majestic
fortress walls of the Acropolis.

Returning back down the hill to Xenomania, try to get a table on the edge of the terrace, where you can enjoy the view over the bay. Here you are, sitting in the middle of Lindos, but far removed from the crowds and din which predominate elsewhere. Dine to the strains of classical music or Flamenco guitar. The restaurant attracts discerning clientele.

After dinner, a visit to the Kioupia bar should round off your evening nicely. To find it, stroll back to the main square and turn into the alley leading uphill to the right just behind the donkey stand. Pass the bars called Sokrátes and Lindos by Night. About 50 paces further on you will find the Kioupia, whose terrace, decorated with Mediterranean plants, is an inviting place to take a seat. Alternatively, go into the bar, where you will find yourself in a restored sea captain's house, decorated with mirrors and Greek amphorae (*kioupia*), which give the bar its name.

Those with plenty of stamina still left may like to visit some of the numerous bars hereabouts, many of them occupying old Lindian houses. Afterwards you may want to head on to the Acropolis disco or the Epos night spot, just out of town, with its bars, nightclub and swimming pool, which is open until the early hours.

A Whole Day Adventure Across the Island

From Lindos via Péfkos to Lárdhos and Láerma; on to Platania and Eleoússa by way of the Foundouklí Monastery; to Profítis Ilías and Embonas, and Tavérna Hasapo; up to Kámiros Skála, and the Artemis Restaurant; then back via Siána, Monólithos, Apolakkiá, Yennádhion and Pilona to Lindos.

From the outset, you should know this is a whirlwind tour, but we will be stopping at villages and also for a swim, so bring your bathing costume. A prerequisite is a reliable car – with a full petrol tank – or a sturdy trail bike. The tour will take you right across the island to the west coast, and since we allow minimum time for the return route, you should be able to squeeze in an additional tour to take in sights on the stretch between Siána and Lindos (if you don't want to rush, plan an overnight stay in Émbonas or Kámiros Skála). Set out as early as possible so that you will not be driving back in the dark.

Leave Lindos via the car park behind the town, and turn down the narrow road for Péfkos. In the morning light, the isolated new hotels look out of place and lost among the barren, rubble covered slopes. However, once you pass the hill beyond Lindos, and get a glimpse of **Péfkos**, you leave this 'touristic desert' behind, and find yourselves surrounded by luxuriant Rhodian veg-

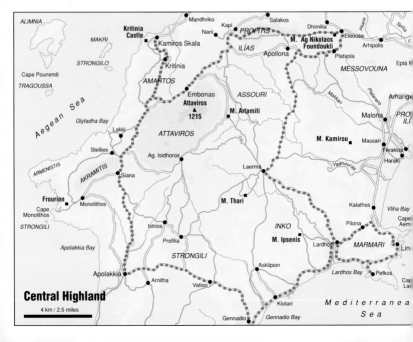

Central Highland

4 km / 2.5 miles

Ruined bridge between Láerma and Apóllona

etation. Péfkos, once a rather out-of-the-way settlement in which
the donkey drivers of Lindos built their homes, is now a growing
resort (it even has a Chinese restaurant and fish and chip shop).
There are plenty of bars, and the nightlife is fast catching up with
that of Lindos. In the village centre, bear right, continuing in the
direction of Lárdhos until you cross over the large coastal road
heading further south. A few metres past this intersection is the
turn-off for the village of **Lárdhos**. The road leads to the centre
of town. A series of cafés here – spruced up for the tourist trade
– are good places for your first, or second breakfast of the morning
(try Anna's Garden). You can count on prices similar to those in
Lindos.

Just behind the village square, follow the sign to Láerma, taking
the road left and inland. Only a few kilometres out of Lárdhos
is evidence of the great forest fire which raged here several years
ago. Up to now, all efforts at reforestation have met with little
success and although some vegetation is gradually growing back,
the charred tree-stumps are a graphic reminder of what can happen
if you toss a match or a burning cigarette away carelessly during
a rainless summer.

Láerma is in the centre of the island and the village, nestled in
the gently rolling hills, has accommodation (used primarily by
visitors to the nearby **Thári Monastery**). There are also several authentic *tavérnes* off the tourist trail. Before reaching the village
centre, head right towards Apóllona. After a few metres, the road
peters out into a dirt track. Unless you're in a four-wheel drive
vehicle, take it easy and drive slowly as you could break an axle.
It's unlikely you will find help easily should you have an accident
in this remote spot. The signs are fewer as the road gets wilder so
if in doubt, go for the widest road.

After about 9km (6 miles) you will notice a watercourse snaking
through eroded stone. Look out for an arch, all that remains of
the ruined bridge here. Follow the road that leads towards the
water (otherwise, you will end up off to the left in mountains

where tree trunks lying across the road make progress impossible). In summer, you can drive through the little stream here without difficulty. In other seasons, check the depth of water before crossing. Be extremely cautious in winter as flash floods in the area often wash the roads away.

The wildest part of the route is now behind you and you can speed up a bit through thinning forest in the direction of **Apóllona**. After about 7km (4 miles) turn off on a road leading right towards **Arhipolis**. From here, continue via the village of **Platania** to **Eleoússa**, where you can stop in the elegant Italianate square. The crumbling facades and arcades lining one of the long sides of the rectangular plaza belong to the governor's palace, dating from the time of the Italian occupation. Nowadays the Greek military has taken up residence; photography of the military headquarters on the square is prohibited.

Italianate plaza in Eleoússa

Finding the way out of town can be puzzling, unless you doggedly follow the signs for **Mt Profítis Ilías (Prophet Elijah)**, at 800m (3,625ft) the third highest mountain on Rhodes. Three kilometres (2 miles) further on you will find the Byzantine chapel of **Ághios Nikólaos Foundouklí** (Saint Nicholas of the Hazelnuts), dating from the 14th century, and remarkable for its magnificent wall paintings. This pretty church probably got its name from the hazel trees that used to grow on this side of the mountain, as *foundouklí* means hazelnut in Greek. There is a magnificent view from the church even if the nut-trees disappeared long ago.

Below the road is a square shaded by plane trees where the former monastery-church celebrated saints' days with both feasting and dancing. On Easter Monday, the residents of the surrounding countryside gather for a pilgrimage to visit the icon of the Virgin Mary of Eleoússa.

The route continues further uphill through a thickly forested area to Mt Profítis Ilías itself. With each kilometre that you travel, the air grows cooler, and you may even see little wisps of fog clinging to the cliffs. You can park in the car park in front of the largest building.

No, this is not a German castle, but two impressive hotels, the Elafos and Elatina ('stag' and 'doe', the island's mascots, which you'll find duplicated on souvenir T-shirts and figurines), built in the alpine style by the Italians. The hotels have have been renovated in recent years and now offer category "A" accommodation, but they are open only during high season. It's quite chilly up here, so after a glance round the game preserve beneath the Elafos Hotel, you'll probably want to drive on.

A short distance uphill the road reaches the summit of the pass and then starts to wind down the other side of the mountain. At the foot of the mountain, a sign to the left points the way to

Alpine style hotels, Mt Profítis Ilías

Émbonas. As well as being the island's premier wine-producing village, Émbonas is known for traditional dancing, particularly by women. Some of the older people still wear local costume as a matter of course, and knitted, woven and lace wares are on sale. These days the village is a popular venue for Greek entertainments, with parties organised by travel agents in Rhodes Town. The dancing is accompanied by copious amounts of locally-produced wine, which soon persuades visitors to join in the irrepressible *syrtáki*. However, for the real thing, visit the village at festival time in August.

If you want to eat here, the Tavérna Hasapo, a restaurant-cum-butcher shop, is recommended for succulent kebabs. It's next to the modern main church. While you're in the village, don't pass up the opportunity to try local wine from the barrel, or the *soúma*, the Rhodian firewater (similar to *grappa*); you can have an empty bottle filled at plenty of places.

Those who prefer seafood to meat should hop back into the car and drive on another 12km (7 miles) to Kámiros Skála on the west coast. If you are not too hungry, turn left into **Kritinía**, founded by the Cretans in around 1500BC and today one of the most atmospheric villages on the island.

From Kritinía, as well as from the main road, you can catch a glimpse of the ramparts of **Kritinía Castle** on the rugged west coast. Located exactly halfway between Kámiros Skála and Kritinia, it offers impressive views inland and of the west coast.

In Kámiros Skála, you will be amply rewarded for your long trek at the **Althameni Restaurant**, to the right of the car park area. At any rate, you will be arriving in the little fishing bay with

Restaurant Artemis in Kámiros Skála

its three restaurants well after the midday rush hour, when the place is flooded with hungry passengers from the tourist buses. Ask the waiters to show you their wide selection of fresh fish and seafood, including giant prawns and lobsters, which are especially recommended, as is the *kalamári*. In comparison to other restaurants on the island, the prices in Kámiros Skála are quite reasonable and may inspire you to return. The schedule allows you to stop here for a leisurely lunch.

Your return route, primarily by way of asphalted roads via **Siána** and **Monólithos** to **Apolakkiá**, proceeds, straight across the interior to **Yennádhion**, with all sorts of interesting intermediary stops along the way (for details of these, see Tour 11: *A Day-long Tour Across Southern Rhodes*). And if you are feeling hot and dusty, you may want to stop off for a swim at the small shingle beach of Fourni, near Monólithos.

Accommodation

Visitors in the high season should expect to find Lindos heavily booked by package tour visitors. From mid-July to mid-August independent travellers who haven't pre-booked will have difficulty finding a free room, as most hotel and pension owners have contracts with package-tour operators.

Some hoteliers do deal solely with independent travellers, but they can be hard to find. Booking in advance through an agency is strongly advised. Both of the following agencies rent villas and studios:

VILLAGE HOLIDAYS
Tel: 2244 031486

LINDOS SUNTOURS
Tel: 2244 031333

To find private rooms in Lindos, your best bet is to look around the eastern quarter of the village. There are a number of basic but reasonable private rooms just off the 'donkey path' – the narrow street that the donkey owners use to carry visitors to the Lindos Acropolis. Failing these, contact the Pallas Travel Office (tel: 2244 031494) in Lindos village.

Restaurants

There are many restaurants in Lindos offering rooftop dining – an experience to savour. The quality is reasonable overall but some places are naturally better than others. Prices tend to be on the whole a little higher than elsewhere on the island, but are worth it for by the very romantic atmosphere.

As the village is small, the restaurants listed here don't have addresses as such. They are generally easy to find; if you can't locate a particular restaurant, just ask around.

ARHONDIKO
Tel: 2244 031 713
An atmospheric restaurant serving international Greek cuisine. Located in a pretty old stone house.

CYPRUS TAVERN
Tel: 2244 031 539
Rhodes' only Cypriot taverna, this restaurant serves typical Cypriot dishes such as *afelia* (beef in tomato sauce with crushed coriander) and *seftalies* (thick, spicy minced meat sausages).

KALYPSO
Tel: 2244 031 669
Housed in an old captain's house with a pretty courtyard and carved walls, Kalypso offers a romantic setting for a special meal. The cooking is top-notch, based on a Rhodian-Greek menu with a few interesting twists.

MARIA'S TAVERNA
Tel: 2244 031 375
This is a good choice for good, hearty cooking and a homely atmosphere without the usual restaurant trappings. Fish and meat based menu. Dinner only.

MVRIKOS
Tel: 2244 031 232
This is one of Lindos' best choices. Excellent fish at moderate prices,. and attentive and friendly service. Located by the main square at the village entrance.

TAVERNA DIONYSUS
Tel: 2244 031 810
With its superb views, this is a great location for rooftop dining, especially in the evening. The long menu offers the full complement of standard Greek specialities.

Bars and Nightlife

Lindos is known for its nightlife, though in actual fact much of this is pleasantly low-key and consists of sitting in cosy small bars or discreet little clubs. Most of these are clustered on the hillside on the west side of the village.

ARCHES NIGHT CLUB

A small, low-key club that doesn't crank up until quite late in the evening. Mixture of Greek and non-Greek music.

CAPTAIN'S HOUSE BAR

Pleasant chill-out bar in a 17th-century house at the upper (eastern) side of the village, where you can hear yourself talk. Can be hard to find, but worth it.

COURTYARD BAR

A popular bar boasting a courtyard. The photographs in the display case outside will give you an idea of the extrovert, party atmosphere that prevails.

LINDOS BY NIGHT

Close to the Courtyard Bar, this is a slightly more sophisticated option, but it can also get pretty lively after midnight.

MUSEUM BAR

Housed in the original Lindos museum, this is a relaxed bar with a cool interior. Gets busy when the UK football is on.

THE LINDIAN HOUSE

Located in a restored captain's house on the main street, this is a busy bar with a pleasant interior and a cosy courtyard.

YIANNIS BAR

A very popular watering hole situated on the main street and impossible to miss. It is good for people-watching and for keeping up with must-see sports fixtures on the large TVs.

Money Matters

There are two banks in the village, both with ATMs. The one near the main square is the more reliable of the two. There are several prominent exchange bureaus along the main street which will convert your pound and dollars into euros for a small commission.

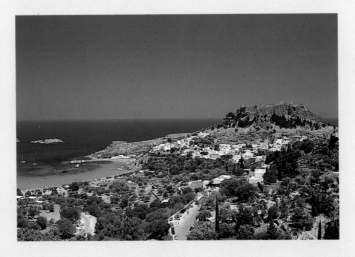

Gennadio

This once rather sleepy village was discovered several years ago by northern European travel agencies. This has led to a dramatic upswing in tourism in the area and the construction of good pensions and hotels in Gennadio (Yennádhio).

The ample sand and gravel beach features several restaurants in addition to sun umbrellas and beach chairs. The quaint and quintessentially Greek village shops have given way to modern, self-service stores in which you will now find a selection of German and British beers alongside the rusks and pulses.

Tour 11

A Day-long Tour Across Southern Rhodes

From Gennadio: breakfast at the Kolossi Café; Lahaniá; Messanagrós; the Skiádhi Monastery and its miraculous icons; a swim en route to Apolakkiá; a visit to the Crusader fortress at Monólithos; Siána; Apolakkiá; Vation; then return to Gennadio.

Begin this tour with a good breakfast on the terrace of the **Kolossi Café** in Gennadio. This popular spot is owned and run by a Greek man and his Greek-American wife, who serve practically anything you could ever dream of for breakfast.

Taking the coastal road from Gennadio, drive for approximately 9km (6 miles) in the direction of Kattavía, until you reach a fork for

Lahaniá. Here turn away from the sea and follow the road until you reach a sign for the village. An arrow to the left shows the way to **Café Platanos**, where the narrow, bumpy road comes to an end. Park the car about 50m (55 yds) away from the village square – really a circle – with a gigantic, shady plane tree in the middle. This square, in contrast to those of other Greek villages, is not located in the heart of town, but instead at one end. The village church, the Café Platanos and the two fountains make a picturesque composition.

Since the 1970s, a great number of foreigners have settled in Lahaniá, buying and restoring the dilapidated houses of this village, which once had a population of 600 citizens. In the 17th century, the village was a notorious pirates' lair.

The village population has now shrunk to about 80 Greek inhabitants and some 50 foreign residents, most of whom are German. Unfortunately, the vintage Greek houses are rented primarily to friends of the owners, so a traveller stranded in Lahaniá will have to seek accommodation in one of the rather scarce private rooms. (Enquire at the Café Platanos or Chrissie's Coffee Shop on the upper main street for further in-

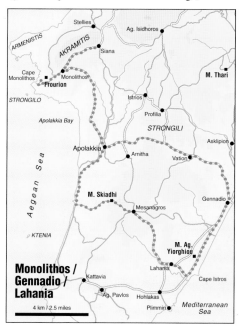

Monolithos / Gennadio / Lahania
4 km / 2.5 miles

The Crusader fortress above Monólithos

formation.) The narrow alleys of Lahaniá are impassable to wheeled traffic and offer a pleasant stroll.

Rejoing the main street of the upper village, turn left, passing the *kafenía*, and exiting Lahaniá on the other side. Just as you put the serpentine stretch up the mountain behind you, follow a road sign to the right towards Messanagrós. The road then turns uphill again, through an area of luxuriant vegetation. After about 10km (6 miles), you will come to the first white houses of this mountain village, where the **chapel** on the outskirts of town is worth a quick visit.

The old-fashioned mountain village of **Messanagrós**, with about 450 inhabitants, was already settled in the 5th century BC. The remains of a small temple here date from this time. On this same site, in years following, an early Christian church was erected. Part of its mosaic, in front of the 15th-century chapel, is still visible. Unfortunately, the rest of the mosaic lies buried under the village road. If you want to view the **Church of the Dormition of the Virgin** – the baptismal font and frescoes are worth seeing – you must find Mike, the proprietor of **Mike's Café Bar**, situated next to the village entrance, and get him to unlock the door for you. Don't forget to leave a couple of euros behind for the upkeep of the church.

At the edge of the village, turn left in the direction of **Kattavía**, and look for an obscure road sign for **Moni Skiádhi** after about 1–2km (½–1 mile). The roads are very rough here and a four-wheel drive vehicle is preferable. Head right along a donkey track uphill for about 1½ km (1 mile, after which switchback bends lead downhill – take this section of the route slowly. About 1km (½ mile) further, you will come to the picturesque **Skiádhi Monastery**, where you will probably be greeted as if you were a long lost friend. The caretakers are always ready to receive visitors, and can sometimes accommodate overnight guests.

The well-kept grounds, with their buildings dating from the 18th and 19th centuries, sprang up around the Church of the Holy Cross, which was erected in the 13th century, then enlarged with a broad nave in the 19th century. The church is famous for its icon of the Panaghía, or Madonna and Child, said to weep tears of blood on its nameday. Legend has it that a 15th-century heretic stabbed the Virgin's cheek, blood flowed from the canvas and the wound and bloodstains are still visible. Over Easter, the church's icons are paraded from village to village until, finally, they come to rest for a whole month on the island of Hálki. On 8 September, when the annual church festival of Skiádi takes place, the Panaghía icons are reverently worshipped by people streaming in from the surrounding region. Afterwards, there is a celebration with live music and dancing, which lasts all night.

Before setting off on the next leg of your trip, to the sea and Apolakkiá, enjoy the wonderful view of the **Koukouliari Mountains** and the west coast while sipping Greek coffee at the monastery.

It's now time for a swim on one of the least spoilt stretches of coastline. When you reach the connecting road between Kattavía and Apolakkiá, turn right and park on one of the paths branching off to the left. Stroll down to the sea for a refreshing swim, but keep in mind that powerful summer breakers produce strong undercurrents in various places on the west coast, and it is advisable not to venture too far out to sea unless you are a really experienced swimmer.

After your swim, it's only a few kilometres on to **Apolakkiá**, where you can stop in the central *platía* and take time for a snack. All four of the *tavérnes* surrounding the square are worth recommending and have kept their prices fairly reasonable.

From the *platía,* follow the road signs to **Monólithos**, the most important village of the region, some 11km (7 miles) further on through luxuriant green forest. Well on the tourist route these days, the monolith is a 236-m (774-ft) high finger of grey rock with a sheer drop to the sea, topped by a Crusader castle. From the main street follow the sign for the **Frourion** (fortress). Just 1km (½ mile) past the village, you'll catch a glimpse of this particularly impressive stronghold, accessed by a precarious stairway.

The breathtaking view makes the hike worthwhile. It begins in a bend in the road beneath the observation point. Once you have arrived you will find, enclosed by the remains of the fortress walls, a little white 15th-century chapel of Ag. Pandelimon with interesting frescoes, the arches of the earlier Chapel of Agros Georgios, and the foundations of a square building. It doesn't require much imagination to see that here the knights could keep track of all shipping moving towards Crete and North Africa.

To reach **Siána**, the next stop on this tour, you must now cut through Monólithos again, retracing your tracks, then drive straight on for about 7km (4 miles). Park your car just behind

the village church next to the **Café-Bar Manos**, and take a look into this typical village *kafenío*, with its enchanting view over the mountainous surrounding landscape. The village is famous for its *soúma*, the local fiery grappa, and four varieties of seasonal honey, which are on sale everywhere. *Soúma*, strongest in the autumn, is distilled from wine residues, and although brewed illegally in many places, by a quirk of history Siána is the only village licensed to produce it. Mystical qualities have been ascribed to it and it's very strong, so don't let your driver try it. Siána honey also has a distinctive flavour and makes a nice gift. Try the flower honey made in spring, thyme in summer, pine in autumn and heather in winter.

You are now ready to start out on the return route, which first leads back to Monólithos and Apolakkiá. On the *platía*, however, do not turn right towards Kattavía. Instead, go left towards Gennadio. Several kilometres further, turn to the right to Arnitha. Then you must bear left, though the road signs do not indicate this. Proceed uphill and, once you have put the summit of the mountain behind you, you are nearing the village of **Vation**, only 7km (4 miles) from Gennadio.

Vation is worth a little side trip. Allow yourself an *oúzo* on the plane tree-shaded village square in the company of elderly villagers before driving back to your accomodation in Gennadio. Here you can still experience something of the friendly composure of unspoilt rural Rhodes.

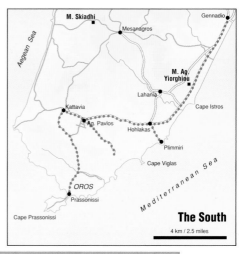

The South

4 km / 2.5 miles

A Day on the Southern Beaches

From Gennadio: sun and swimming at Hawaii Beach; Cape Prassoníssi; Greek coffee at Kattavía; a seafood meal at Plimmíri. This tour is dedicated primarily to the pleasures of swimming, sunning and relaxing under the southern sun.

Start out from Gennadio in the direction of Kattavía (if you are in need of a generous breakfast before setting off, try Klimis, on the beach at Gennadio). After roughly 16km (10 miles), having passed the point where the road branches off towards Plimmíri, you will notice, on the left, two avenues which were laid out by the Italians. This was once the settlement of **Ághios Pavlos**, the location of a prison dating from the Italian occupation, now used today as a pig farm. Turn into the first of the two avenues and drive along the country road towards the sea, until the route peters out into sparsely vegetated sand dunes. Behind the dunes, you will see a broad, sandy beach, usually deserted. If you start out from here and hike to the right along the beach (*not* barefoot), after about 10 minutes you will reach the end of the elongated bay, a spot protected from the wind and shaded by cliffs, a good place to spend an hour or two swimming and sunbathing.

The southern tip of Rhodes: Prassoníssi

Continuing on from Ághios Pavlos, follow the main road for about 3km (2 miles) in the direction of **Kattavía**. Keep to the left at the fork just outside the village. Some 100m/yds further on you will see a road sign for **Prassoníssi** (Leek Island), pointing off to the left on a 7km- (4 mile-) long gravel road to the southern tip of the island. This is where west and east coasts meet. The strong wind which blows here most of the time produces strong breakers, attracting experienced surfers.

You will also find two *tavérnes* serving fresh fish at the narrow isthmus to the little peninsula which stretches out beyond Prassoníssi. For the time being, you should deny yourself another meal and, instead, depending on the weather (the sandy connecting spit is sometimes flooded), take a half-hour stroll to the lighthouse on the other side of the peninsula. However, do not attempt to

Fishing boat in Plimmíri bay

cover this distance by car since it's quite possible you'll get stuck in the sand. A motorcycle is more suitable, if you don't fancy the walk.

Back at the fork in the main road, you can either turn off to the right towards Plimmíri, or drive straight ahead and pay a brief visit to the village of **Kattavía**. After 200m/yds, you will find yourself in the central *platía*, which is flanked by several *kafenía*. At the **Café Tofos**, you can take a seat in the shade of an old tree and study the languid village life of the residents who have, for the

Church in Plimmíri

most part, been spared the ravages of tourism. The only variation in the texture of village life is brought about by the military who are stationed in the area.

Since you are likely to be rather hungry by now, drive 8km (5 miles) back down the main road to the fork for **Plimmíri**, which is at the end of a 1.5km (1 mile) long side street. The outstanding fish restaurant here, Yannis Galantomos, and the romantic view over the little fishing bay, on which a longer swimming beach is located, are probably going to detain you a little longer in Plimmíri.

If you walk up to the hills behind the restaurant, you will come across a collection of ruined homes dating from the German occupation. To the right of these, the ancient city of **Kyrbe** is said to have stood. However, it fell victim to a flood (Greek: *plimmíra*), hence the name of the current village lying below. A later village believed to have existed here was called Ixiá.

The church, which is located just behind the restaurant, was erected on top of the foundation walls of a considerably earlier Christian basilica, whose columns and marble work have been incorporated into the present building. In the front yard of the church is a pond which was once the site of a spring said to have miraculous powers.

A Motorcycle Tour of the Southern Coast

A half-day tour from Gennadio: to Kiotári; Asklipíon; the Thári Monastery; Láerma; and Lárdhos.

Leave the village of **Gennadio** on the coast road heading north. Pass a petrol station and continue on to the intersection for **Asklipíon** (left) and **Kiotári** (right). Bearing right, you will find a beach as beautiful as the one at Haráki. Pull off the road and take a swim. Although many well situated restaurants can be found here, Stefanos (on the left) serves the best fish. If it is late morning and you are

Laerma / Asklipion / Lardhos

4 km / 2.5 miles

ready for an early lunch, ask to see the day's catch; Rhodes is especially famous for its red mullet, swordfish and lobster.

Stay on the coast road for **Asklipíon**, where the oldest church on the island draws many Greek tourists. The Byzantine **Church of the Dormition of the Virgin** was built in 1060 and has some fine 17th-century frescoes. If it is closed, ask at the *kafenio* for the key.

Named after Asklepios, the god of healing, the village stands on the site of the island's ancient medical centre and even now sick pilgrims come to pray at the church. It's a fascinating village and many people still bake their bread in the village's communal oven.

Above the village brood the ruins of a medieval fortress, known locally as **Ioannis Castle**, one of the most southerly strongholds of the knights. The walk up takes about 15-minutes: just follow the track from the public toilets.

Leave the village via one of the upper streets, and head northwest for about 7km (4 miles) via the road for **Láerma**. This will take you through a forest. Two kilometres (1 mile) before you reach Láerma, is **Moni Thári (Thári Monastery)**, one of the island's most precious treasures. Legend has it that a Byzantine princess, afflicted with a fatal illness, had this monastery built so that she might retreat to the wilderness and there die in peace. The monastery was duly built, and the princess miraculously recovered. The picturesque buildings were probably erected between the 9th and 13th centuries, although the foundations date from pre-Christian times. Thári is famous for its frescoes. Some walls have four layers of paintings spanning the 12th–18th centuries and the apse has fine paintings dating from the 12th–16th centuries. Look out for the apostles in shades of red, ochre, black and cream, and on the right wall the head of a dappled horse, probably part of a painting of St George.

A huge annual festival is held here every June. Thousands of people from all over Rhodes and elsewhere gather here to feast and dance the night away. From the monastery, proceed in the direction of **Láerma**, where several *kafenía* will tempt you in for a refreshing pause. Try a Greek 'spoon sweet', *glykó koutalioú,* with your coffee. Continue on towards **Lárdhos**. Ask for directions to the workshop of Lynn Fischer, whose ceramics represent a departure from most ware to be found on Rhodes.

Accommodation

The only travel agency in town has now closed down. For accomodation try the hotels below:

HOTEL CHRISTIANA
Tel: 2244 043228
In the centre of town.

BETTY STUDIOS AND APARTMENTS
In the centre of town.

DENNIS BEACH STUDIOS
Located outside the town centre on the beach.

GOLDEN SUNRISE
Tel: 2244 043003
In the centre of town.

Restaurants

KLIMIS
Beach location, with an attractive terrace, and quite good food.

ANTONIS
Tel: 2244 043300.
Also on the beach, with a beautiful terrace, and outstanding food.

ADAM'S
Tel: 2244 043180

Cafés and Bars

CAFÉ MEMORIES

KOLOSSOS
On the main street.

Vehicle Rental

OASIS CAR RENTAL
Tel: 2244 043168

TEO RENT-A-CAR
Lahania
Tel: 2244042290

Motorcycles can be hired from:
DHIMITRI'S RENT-A-MOTO
Tel: 2224 043064

EXPLORER RENT-A-MOTO
Tel: 2244 043062

Medical Station

There is a medical station (tel: 2244 043233) on the coast road at the entrance to the village.

International Newspapers

DESARIO
Located in the village centre. Tel: 2244 043033.

Dining Experiences

There are several types of eateries in Greece ranging from restaurants with international menus to *psistariá*, *tavérnes* specialising in roasts and barbecues to order. *Tavérnes* are open for lunch and dinner and usually have an array of ready-cooked oven dishes to choose from, such as *laderá*, vegetables or meat stews in rich olive oil and tomato sauce; *stifádho*, a spicy stew of beef or rabbit; *moussaká*, layers of aubergine with potato and minced lamb topped with bechamel sauce; and *pastítisio*, macaroni baked with mince. They may also offer pork cutlets, roast lamb and *souvláki*, kebabs of pork, chicken or lamb on a skewer. Roast chicken is usually delicious and often free-range.

Vegetarians are reasonably well served with *yígantes*, giant butter beans in tomato sauce; *fasolákia*, green string beans; *briám*, a mix of aubergine, courgette and tomatoes rather like *ratatouille*; *hórta*, local greens tossed in oil and lemon; and delicious *tirópites* or *spanakópites,* cheese or spinach pies in light *filo* pastry.

Fish appears on most menus and is generally quoted per kilogram, not per portion. The fish favoured by Greeks, and the most expensive, are *barboúnia* (red mullet) and swordfish. Cheaper and delicious if fresh (though sometimes chewy if frozen) are *kalamária* (fried squid) and grilled octopus. In season, small fish such as whitebait, *merídha* and *atherina* are cheap and tasty.

In the tourist centres, international food tends to dominate menus, and pizza and peppered steak feature regularly. In Rhodes Town, fast food restaurants have crowded out the traditional *gíros* and *souvláki* stands. The use of microwave ovens has now

become so widespread that dishes which were traditionally served at room temperature now burn your tongue.

Rhodes has a wide range of restaurants with Mexican, Cantonese, Indian, French, Italian, Scandinavian and British eating places, all competing for custom. Complementing this variety are some exceptional Greek *tavérnes,* offering imaginative Greek cuisine and fine international restaurants in the luxury hotels.

Tipping customs are as follows: in addition to the service charge which is included in the price of a meal, a 5–10 percent tip should be left for the waiter. Also, it is customary to leave something for the assistant waiter who brings the bread and clears the dishes.

Beverages

On any occasion, as an aperitif, after meals, as well as in between, *oúzo*, a liqueur flavoured with anise, is popular. In the country-side it is drunk undiluted, taken in sips alternating with sips of cold water. In the city, it is often served with ice or mixed with cold water. A little glass of *oúzo* consumed at the appropriate time settles the stomach and calms the mind. In the *kafenía,* it is usually served by the glass or in a *karafáki,* small carafe. Unfortunately, the custom of serving *mezédhes,* morsels of cucumber and cheese,

olives or nuts, with *oúzo* is dying out in most tourist areas.

Greek coffee is consumed either *glykó* (sweet), *métrio* (medium) or *skéto* (without sugar). Sugar is not served on the side, but boiled with the coffee. The grounds remain at the bottom of the cup as you drink, and should stay there.

Wine is normally dry, but varieties designated 'demi-sec' are sweet. The wines offered in most restaurants come from the large bottling firms of Caïr and Emery. Caïr distributes the Ilios (white) and Chevalier (red) labels as well as the expensive white, red and rosé Moulin. Emery wines also come in white, red and rosé. Look out for the excellent crisp white Villare and the newer red Mythiko. Tsantalis from Northern Greece is also highly recommended. Beyond Caïr and Emery, some table wines worth recommending are the Calliga, Boutari, Nemea and Apelia labels. Retsína, or resin flavoured wine, is less than half the price of non-resinated, but it's an acquired taste. **Kourtaki** is an old favourite and comes in flip-top half bottles, but you may prefer the local **Caïr**, which has a more delicate flavour.

Beer is well on the way to pushing aside wine on the Greek table. Among the beers produced under licence, such as Henninger, Löwenbräu, Amstel and Heineken, the last leads the pack. The Greek beer Mythos is becoming popular.

Shopping

Rhodes has stocked its supermarket shelves to meet the requirements of visitors from the north. In all the larger stores you will find the products you use at home. In Faliráki, the shopkeepers have gone the whole hog and you can now see fake Safeways, ASDA etc shop signs over little local supermarkets, the logos pinched from British carrier bags! Furthermore, there are off licences everywhere, though their prices have rocketed in recent years. Still, purchasing spirits on Rhodes is worth your while, since alcoholic beverages are still around 20–30 percent cheaper than in much of the rest of Europe.

Tobacco products are a similar bargain for visitors. A carton of cigarettes made under Greek licence (Marlboro, Camel etc) costs about 40 percent less on Rhodes than in Britain, for example. Even more reasonably priced are rough domestic cigarettes such as Assos, and Karellia.

Souvenirs

In Rhodes City you will find **jewellery** shops on every corner where distinctive 'Greek gold' designs sell for comparatively reasonable prices. Of course, the art of gold working has a long tradition on Rhodes, though most of the jewellery sold on the island today is produced in Italy.

The Athens based jeweller **Ilias**

Lalaounis maintains a shop on the former Auberge de l'Auvergne, where flawless copies of ancient designs and collections featuring Byzantine elements, rock crystal or pavé diamonds may tempt you.

The **Ministry of Culture** shop on the corner of the Street of the Knights specialises in replicas or artefacts from the museum. The statues, etc are sold with certificates of authentication.

In the city, **leathers and furs** are also offered for sale. This may seem rather peculiar considering the often sweltering heat. One of the best shops is **Dano Niko**, 92 Sokrátous Street, which also stocks vibrant kilims made in the village of Émbonas.

Ceramics, embroidery and woven carpets are also traditional Rhodian products, but the quality is variable.

Hand-painted ceramics can be found at **Phidias**, on Panetou Street. The motifs on this ware are based on ancient patterns

though more modern designs are also available. Equally worthy of mention are **O Myrina**, on Griva Street, where you can also buy ceramic figurines, and the **Greek Gallery**, 74 Sokrátous Street. Rhodian ceramics it should be noted, are famous throughout Greece. Traditional designs are outlined in black on a white or cream background, then hand-painted in bold colours. Lamps and huge platters will add stunning accents to monochrome rooms back home. Located in the area of Arhángelos is the **pottery workshop** of **Panaghiotis**, who produces amphorae in the old style, pots and bowls, and other ware. His ceramics are unpainted for the most part, but the simple, pleasing shapes of his everyday articles are decoration enough. Right on the main road as you enter the village of Arhángelos is the **Neofitou Ceramic Manufactory**, where you can obtain fine copies of ancient ceramics.

You can purchase **handmade lace** most reasonably in Líndhos, where this art has long been practised. In Arhángelos and Afándou, you can buy beautifully made woven **carpets and runners** at remarkably low prices, as well as handmade traditional **boots**. In Siána, a small mountain village on the west coast, you can obtain superior quality **honey** and *soúma*, a homemade grape spirit which comes close in taste to Italian *grappa*. You can buy **wine** in bulk at Émbonas. Also located here is the largest wine company in the region, Emery.

Travel Essentials

Travel To and From Rhodes

The most comfortable and convenient waxy to get to Rhodes is by air. Rhodes is linked to the UK and Europe by seasonal charter flights or by Olympic Airways from London and cities in the United States via Athens. Rhodes is linked by Olympic Airways to many domestic destinations including Thessaloniki, Iraklio and Santorini. Aegean Airlines also flies to Rhodes from Athens and Thessaloniki.

Domestic ferry services link Rhodes with Piraeus (Athens) and many intermediate islands in the Cyclades and Dodecanese. There are both 'Superfast' and regular services. Ticket prices on the Superfast services are more expensive than on the ordinary services. A daily catamaran links Rhodes with Marmaris in Turkey.

Rhodes Airport is 16km (10 miles) from Rhodes Town. It has money exchange counters that are open to meet most incoming flights, as well as ATMs.

There is no Olympic Airways bus from the airport to Rhodes Town. There is, however, a regular scheduled bus services which stops on the main road outside the air terminal. The ticket costs €1.70. The last bus for Rhodes Town leaves at 11.45pm.

A taxi from the airport into Rhodes Town costs roughly €13–14 dependir on the time of day and the amount luggage you have. If another passeng turns up going the same way as yo do not be surprised when the ta driver charges you both the full fare

If you arrive by ferry, it's just short walk into the Old Town, but th can be difficult if you have heavy bag There are plenty of taxis from her into the New Town, but they may refu to take you into the medieval quart on account of the narrow streets.

Customs and Duties

Since the abolition of duty-fr allowances for EU countries, all goo brought into Greece from Britain ar Ireland must be duty-paid. If you a coming from outside the EU, the dut free allowances on tobacco, alcohol ar perfumes are as follows: 200 cigarett or 50 cigars or 250 grammes of toba co; 1 litre of spirits or 4 litres of win 250 ml of cologne or 50 ml of perfum Other valuable items brought in fro non-EU countries may be subject to in port duties or may be simply entere into your passport so that you a obliged to take them with you whe you leave. In practice checks are rare carried out, though these can be mo stringent for visitors entering Gree from Turkey.

Changes in Booking

hanges in booking for charter flight
cket holders can usually be handled
y the individual carrier's agents in
hodes City. A prerequisite for chang-
g your ticket is the availability of a
orresponding seat on another aircraft.
ou must pay the communication costs
curred and a re-booking fee.

If your efforts to re-book prove fruit-
ss and it is a case of emergency or
lness, you can try to re-book your
ight at the airport check-in counter
f your carrier. If there is a seat avail-
ble on one of your carrier's aircraft
due to a no-show perhaps), then the
irport manager may give you permis-
ion to leave without changing your
icket, but only upon the presentation
f a legal affidavit stating the nature
f your problem.

Money Matters

Banks

Aany banks now have ATMs from which
ou can withdraw cash at any time.
here are also some stand-alone ATMs
round Rhodes.

Currency

he Greek monetary unit is the euro.
here are 1, 2, 5, 10, 20 and 50 cent
oins, known as *lepta* in Greek, as well
s 1 and 2 euro coins. Banknotes come
n denominations of €5, €10, €20,
€50, €100, €200, €500 and €1,000.
Greek issued euro coins have different
lesigns to their counterparts in other
art of the euro zone. Coins from other
uro zone countries are legal tender in
Greece. Bank notes are the same in all
uro zone countries

Climate and Geography

Time Zones

Greek time (EMT) is two hours ahead
f Greenwich Mean Time. Greek sum-
ner time is EMT plus one hour.

Air Temperatures

On Rhodes, summer does not arrive
until May, when an average of 25°C
(77°F) prevails. June, at almost 30°C
(86°F), is considerably hotter, but August, when the mercury reaches a high
of around 33°C (91°F), is blistering.
Visitors should bring sunblock, and
wear hats and long sleeves to avoid
dangerous burns even in spring.

In September, June

temperatures return, and October temperatures are similar to those of May.
January and February, when the temperature averages around 16°C (61°F),
are easily the coldest months of the
year. Statistics for the island record
peak temperatures of over 40°C (104°F)
and lows of nearly freezing.

Sea Temperatures

You will rarely see a Greek in the sea
before the beginning of June, in other
words not until the water temperature
reaches about 21°C (70°F). Tourists
arriving from cooler countries are not
so sensitive: they jump into the water

in May, when the water temperature is 19°C (66°F). By August the water has warmed to about 25°C (77°F), so a dip in the sea is no longer bracing. In October, the temperature sinks again to about 22°C (72°F) and reaches the lowest levels of the year in February and March: 16°C (61°F).

Wind

When the weather is hot, from May till September, but particularly from mid-July to mid-August, the wind known as the *meltémi* blows in from the north to cool brows and tempers. It blows primarily between morning and sunset, and can reach a wind strength of 5 or 6 on the Beaufort

Scale. If it reaches 7 or more it will disrupt hydrofoil and ferry schedules as by law the port police are supposed to prohibit all shipping from leaving port for safety reasons. At its strongest it can whisk glasses and bottles off *tavérna* tables and even send chairs hurtling. However, on the whole, visitors are grateful for the cooling effects of this summer breeze. The west coast is particularly exposed, hence the serried ranks of umbrellas acting as windbreaks on the beaches.

In antiquity, Aeolos, the son of the sea god Poseidon, was considered the creator of the *meltémi*. Today, it is

known that strong air pressure grad‐ ents between the western and easter‐ Mediterranean produce these vigoro‐ air movements.

Rainfall

From the beginning of June until th end of August rain is practically un‐ heard of. April and May average thr‐ rainy days; October averages six.

In December and January you wi‐ need real rainwear. With about 18 rain days per month, there's little chan‐ of getting a decent tan.

Forest Fires

It is a sad fact of everyday life on th island that each and every summer the‐ will be small, and larger, field and fore‐ fires. However, several years ago almo‐ one-quarter of the forest area of Rhod‐ was destroyed by a huge fire that c‐ right across the island. Tragically, th cause of the fire has never been deter‐ mined. Although even a splinter of gla‐ lying in the right place can cause a fi‐ if the sun hits it at the correct angl‐ the most common causes of forest fire‐ are carelessness and arson. The fir‐ watch, which was instituted after th great island fire, is designed to spo‐ and fight potential forest fires. The fir‐ watch 'brigade' is spread over the entir‐ island and members are in constant ra‐ dio contact so that trucks and plane‐ can be called in immediately to dous‐ the flames. Once a fire has occurred‐ however, the damage is usually irrepara‐ ble. As a result, the erosion of the i‐ land's soil escalates, promotin‐ catastrophic flooding, such as the villag‐ of Lárdhos has experienced since th‐ great forest fire. Greek environmenta‐ activists have contributed much throug‐ private initiatives and voluntar‐ labour to the reforestation of a portio‐ of the burned woodland.

When camping and walking, holiday‐ makers should exercise the greatest pos‐ sible caution to avoid causing fires.

Getting Around

Ferry Connections

Regular ferries operate to other islands in the Dodecanese group and the Aegean, Piraeus, Thessaloníki and Marmaris. Details and reservations from all travel agencies or from Dane Sea Lines, 92 Odos Australias, tel: 2241 077 078; www.dane.gr.

There are also day-cruises to Lindos and the south of the island, Symi, Kós and Marmaris. For further information contact the Dodecanese Tourism Office (Mon–Fri 8am–3pm), corner of Makariou and Papago, Rhodes Town, tel: 2241 023655/2241 023255; email: eot-rodos@otenet.gr.

Visiting Turkey

It used to be the case that travellers arriving in Greece on charter flights from Europe could not visit Turkey for longer than a day without running the risk of invalidating their return flight. This is no longer the case. Visitors may visit Turkey freely on day trips and longer stays. Check with your local Turkish consulate or Turkish tourist office for the latest visa regulations. Visas for US and EU citzens are normally issued on the spot – for a hefty fee – at the Turkish port of disembarkation. Day-trippers do not require Turkish visas, but must pay Turkish port taxes in addition to the ferry fare. These taxes are normally built into the price of the day trip fare, at the time of writing around €30.

Taxis

The central taxi stand in Rhodes City is on the Platia Rimini in Mandhráki.

Bus Connections

Rhodes has a well-developed bus network which connects all villages with Rhodes City. The timetable varies according to the season. The central bus terminal in Rhodes City is in the Néa Agorá in Mandhráki where bus schedules are posted.

For information on services outside the capital, you can phone 2241 027206 for buses to eastern Rhodes or 2241 026300 for buses to western Rhodes. Within Rhodes City, call KTEL: 27706.

Vehicle Rental

In Rhodes City, you will find representatives of all the big international car rental firms, including Hertz, Avis and Inter-rent, whose prices for their smallest models are standardised and currently stand at about €40 per day (double this for large saloons or jeeps). Local firms offer their vehicles at substantially cheaper rates, particularly off season when competition between companies is fierce. If you waive a receipt and take the car for several weeks, you can get rates of around €25 per day off season.

The disadvantages of renting from Greek firms is that their vehicles are sometimes in poor condition, and you are usually barred from using them off paved roads. Check that you are fully insured before you set off. Some companies won't cover damage to the underside of the vehicle, so if you plan to go on rough tracks be extra careful or hire a 4-wheel drive.

Motorcycles and scooters can be rented in all the main resorts. Rates start at around €12 for 50cc. Larger motorbikes, up to 1,100cc, are available from a few companies (try Sky or Rent-a-Harley in Rhodes City). A full motorbike licence is required for vehicles larger that 50cc. A crash helmet (supplied) is compulsory.

Mountain bikes and plain push-bikes can be rented for approximately €3 per day.

Bear in mind that the accident rate involving two-wheeled vehicles is phenomenal, so drive with extreme caution at all times.

Traffic Regulations

Although locals appear to take little notice of many traffic rules, foreigners should follow them as best they can. In the event of an accident, tourists are at an extreme disadvantage because of language difficulties. The speed limit in urban/suburban areas and villages is 50kph (30mph). On main roads 80kph (50mph). The wearing of seat belts is compulsory.

The allowable blood alcohol level is 0.05 percent. Police checks are sporadically carried out and offenders are arrested on the spot, and held until trial before a magistrate, which is usually the next day. Anyone driving with more than 0.05 percent of alcohol in their blood is liable to a minimum two months imprisonment or a very stiff fine, plus court costs.

Fuel

Service stations are found throughout the island. Many close at 7pm and on Sunday and public holidays. The price of petrol is considerably lower than it is in the UK and in some other European countries, but quite a bit higher than in the US.

Diesel is roughly €0.20 cheaper than unleaded fuel, which currently retails in Rhodes for around €0.83 per litre. Diesel, unleaded and leaded fuel are widely available. Car owners use vehicle diesel *(petrelaio kinisis)* as opposed to heating diesel *(petrelaio thermansis)*. The latter is cheaper (by about 45 percent) and can only legally be sold for use in domestic heaters. Its use – legal or otherwise – in vehicles, while technically feasible, is not recommended as it does not contain the additives needed by modern vehicle diesel engines.

Health and Emergencies

EU citizens are entitled to free medical treatment providing they have obtained and had validated an E111 form before leaving their home country. However it is recommended that you also take out health/accident insurance, which should also cover the cost of repatriation, if necessary.

Pharmacies / Chemists

Chemists are found on most city streets and in major resort villages. Hours Monday, Tuesday, Thursday and Friday 8am–1pm and 5–9pm; on Wednesday and Saturday, they close at 2pm. Details of night chemists, open on a rota basis are listed in every pharmacy window (or tel: 107). Most chemists speak some English

Many medicines that are only available under prescription in other European countries are available over the counter in Greece. These include Prozac and antibiotics.

Hospitals

Rhodes General Hospital, Red Cross Street, Rhodes Town.
First Aid: 2241 080000. In Rhodes Town: 166

Medical Centres

Faliráki: tel: 2241 085555
Afándou: tel: 2241 051393
Arhángelos: tel: 2241 022400
Lindos: tel: 2244 031224
Lárdhos: tel: 2244 044347

Police

Crimes are relatively rare on Rhodes Ordinary police wear a green uniform and deal with traffic offences and may impose fines for speeding and vehicle checks. The Tourist Police is a branch of the force that deals with tourist problems; found mainly in Rhodes New Town and the larger resorts; they speak English and wear a dark grey uniform
Emergency, tel: 100
Non-emergency, tel: 2241 023849
Tourist Police, tel: 2241 035945
Harbour Police, tel: 2241 027695

Embassies & Consulates

Australian Embassy and Consulate, 37D Soutsou Street, 115 21 Athens. Tel: 2106 450404.

British Embassy and Consulate, 1 Ploutarchou Street, 106 75 Athens. Tel: 2107 236211.

British Consulate, Rhodes, Pavlou Mela 3, Rhodes New Town, 85100 Rhodes. Tel: 2241 027247.

Canadian Embassy, 4 Gennadiou Street, 115–21 Athens. Tel: 2107 232 771/2.

Irish Embassy, 7, Vass. Konstantinou Avenue, 106 74 Athens. Tel: 2107 232771/2.

New Zealand General Consulate, 24 Xanias Street, 115 28 Athens. Tel: 2106 874700.

South African Embassy and Consulate, 60 Kifisias Avenue, 151 27 Athens. Tel: 2106 806645.

Turkey, Polytehniou 10, Rhodes. Tel: 2241 23362.

US Embassy and Consulate, 91 Vas Sofias Avenue, 115 27 Athens. Tel: 2107 212951.

Post and Communications

Post

Main Post Office
Mandraki, Odhós Eleftherías, Rhodes City, tel: 2241 22212. Hours: Monday to Friday 7am–8.30pm.

In addition, postage stamps can be bought at kiosks and stationers.

Telephone

There are very few coin-operated phones in Rhodes. Pre-pay cardphones are the norm and can be found all over the island. They take pre-paid phone cards which can be bought at street kiosks *(periptera)*. Some have flat top card phones while others have regular phones. Just make your call and pay the kiosk owner. The cost of your call is calculated on a meter inside the kiosk.

Mobile phone users will probably be able to use their phones on a roaming agreement with their home mobile phone company and one of the Greek mobile phone companies. Calls from your phone are charged at local rates, but calls to your phone incur the cost of the international call from your home country. A good solution is to take out a local pay-as-you-go mobile number for around €15–20 for a simple start up kit *(paketo syndesis)*.

US and Canadian mobile phone owners will only be able to roam or take out a local number if they have dual band handsets.

The local international access code is 00. Add to that your destination country code plus the subscriber number (minus any initial zeros) and you're connected. Some common destination country codes are Canada (1), Australia (61), United States (1), United Kingdom (44).

All Greek phone numbers are 10-digit and include an area code. All 10 digits must be dialled, even for local calls. The first four digits indicate the local area. Greek mobile phone numbers are also 10-digit. The first two numbers are always 69.

Radio

Radio ERT 2 broadcasts English language news at 2.25pm daily.

Festivals and Holidays

National Holidays

25 March, Independence Day. On this day in 1821 the revolt against Turkish rule began. The day is celebrated with military and school parades.

28 October, Óhi Day. On this day in 1940, the Greek government defied Mussolini's ultimatum demanding capitulation without resistance. Because of this historic 'no', the day is called Óhi Day.

Religious Festivals

Greek Orthodox Easter is undoubtedly the most important festival of the year; it is usually celebrated in April but occasionally in May. The high point of the festival is Easter Mass at midnight on Easter Saturday/Sunday.

23 April, Ághios Yiórghios, celebrated at Kritinía.

Beginning of June, great monastery festival at Moni Thári.

24 June, Summer Solstice, marked by many island celebrations.

29 June, SS Petros and Pavlos, special festivities are held at St Paul's Bay at Líndhos.

17 July, Aghia Marina, at Paradissi.

20 July, Profítis Ilías, in front of Ilías Church on Mt Profítis Ilías.

27 July 27, Ághios Pandelimonas, at Siána.

29/30 July, Ághios Soulas at St Silas at Soroní with competitive events and donkey races.

6 August, Metamorfosis, at Maritsa.

14-23 August, Panaghía Festival at Kremastí.

15 August, Dormition of the Virgin, celebrated throughout Greece.

8 September, Festival of the Holy Virgin at Moni Tsambika, Moni Skiádhi and Émbonas.

18 September, Ághios Loukas held at Afándou.

Holiday Surcharges

From Christmas until 6 January, as we as during the Easter period, *tavérne* restaurants, and taxi drivers demand 'bonus' (*dhóro*). This amounts to abo €0.80 in taxis and 10 percent extra restaurants.

Photography

Rhodes is extremely photogenic and t majority of people come armed with camera. In the larger villages colo negative as well as slide film is availab The prices are, however, between on third and 50 percent higher than northern Europe and America. It therefore a good idea to bring sufficie quantities of film along with you. It no longer necessary to protect film fro fogging in a lead pouch when passir through customs.

Etiquette

Salutations

In Greek cities, as elsewhere in the 'd veloped' West, people pass on the stre without greeting one another. Howeve in Rhodes' villages, such pleasantri are an integral part of daily life, ar even visitors should greet locals if the want to avoid causing offence.

From dawn until about 3pm, or says *Kaliméra* (good day). (*Kalimér sas* is the polite/plural form.) Unt nightfall, upon arriving, and unt about 8pm upon departing, it is cu tomary to say *Kalispéra (Kalispéra sas* On the other hand, one would sa *Kaliníhta* upon arriving after midnig and on departure after 8pm.

If all this is too complicated master, simply say *Yássou* (familiar singular form) or *Yássas* (polite/plur form). See *The Greek Language*, pag 91, for a lengthier introduction to bas Greek. If you master the rudiment and Rhodians will be both surprise and pleased.

Nudism

There are no official nudist beaches on Rhodes. As a rule, the Greeks are conservative in such matters and offended by blatant nudity. Nevertheless, topless bathing takes place on all the larger beaches, and women need no longer fear being arrested for wearing only the bottom half of their bikini – not uncommon a few decades ago. On beaches in the south, which are usually semi-deserted, you can skinny dip with confidence, as long as there are no Greek families in the vicinity. Bathing costumes are strictly for the beach, and you should cover up even to visit a beach restaurant.

Sport

Golf

There is an eight-hole golf course at Afándou which stages the Rodhos Open Tournament in October. Information may be obtained by checking the website www.afandougolfcourse.com.

Underwater Sports

From the beginning of May through to the end of October scuba diving is very popular in Rhodes. However, the sport is prohibited in Greece unless divers are accompanied by diving school instructors. Diving for artefacts in the waters off Rhodes is strictly forbidden and is a punishable offence.

The following three companies offer diving services to beginners and advanced divers alike:

Dive Med College, Lisavonas 33, tel: 2241 061115, fax: 2241 066584.
Waterhoppers, Kritika 45, tel/fax: 2241 038146.
Scuba Diving Trident School, Zervou 2, tel/fax: 2241 029160.

Windsurfing

The west coast at Ixia and Vliha Bay near Líndhos offer good conditions. Experienced windsurfers like Cape Prassonissi, on the southern tip of the island. Further details from the Tourist Offices.

Sailing

Details on sailing are available at Rhodes Yacht Club, Rhodes City, Platia Kountouriou 9, tel: 2241 0232877.

Tennis

Most of the large luxury hotels in Rhodes City have tennis courts, which are accessible to the general public for a fee.

Riding

Mike's Horses (9am–1pm, and 4–8pm. The stables are on the road to Ialyssós/Filerimos.

Culture

Theatre

In summer (Apr–Oct), a Sound and Light show takes place every night near the Néa Ágora. Performances in English are at 9.15pm (Mon, Wed, Fri) and 11.15pm (Tues, Thur, Sun); one hour earlier from 1 September to 31 October.

In the Old Town, Greek Folk Dances are presented daily, except Saturday, at 9.15pm in Platía Póli during summer.

The current programme of the Rhodian National Theatre is available at the Tourist Information office.

Museums

In general, the museums on Rhodes are open Tues–Sun 8.30am–3pm, closed Monday. Admission is free on Sunday.

Since the crush of visitors is heavy, doors may be shut in your face by 2pm. This applies particularly to the Acropolis of Líndhos.

Religion

Places of Worship

Roman Catholic churches: Both Santa Maria and San Francisco are open continuously.

Mosques: On Friday evening Muslims meet for prayer in the Suleiman Paşa Mosque on Odhós Sokrátous.

Jewish Synagogue: The Synagog Shalom, near Platía Evreon, is op continuously.

Useful Information

Snakes

There are snakes on Rhodes, but t majority of these are non-poisonou Vipers are the only snakes whose bi can be dangerous, but snake bite ca be treated immediately at any medic station. Viper bites are unusual sin the snakes tend to slip away at t slightest vibration of approaching fee In May and June you may al encounter snakes in the villages, sin they like to lay their eggs where the is masonry and this is the time for re ovations. This is no reason to nurtu exaggerated fears, as snakes are afra of people.

Toilets

On occasion, the hygienic standard Rhodian plumbing leaves much to desired, although the traditional Turkis style squat-toilet has been replace almost everywhere by western fixture (There's a lot to be said – by physicia – for the former system, but this is n the place to elaborate.) Since there no mains drainage on Rhodes, toil paper (and all other paper waste) shoul be thrown into the bin provided. Som times, tourists complain that these pa are overflowing, but if you consid the difficulty of waste disposal and t numbers of visitors who descend on t island in summer, perhaps you will a little more understanding.

The Greek Language

If you take the trouble to learn son Greek prior to embarking on your vis to Rhodes, you will be rewarded wit praise and will make friends more easil It is a great help to learn the Greek a phabet, even if the majority of stree signs are also written in Roman letter

You should have a dictionary and a language guide handy. The *lingua franca* in the tourism sector is English, though German is quickly gaining ground.

Greek is a phonetic language. There are some combinations of vowels and consonants which stand for certain sounds, and some slight pronunciation changes determined by what letter follows but, generally, sounds are pronounced as they are written, without additions or omissions. Learning the phonetic values of the Greek alphabet, and then reading, say, street signs out loud, is a good way to get the feel of the language.

Many people on Rhodes have some knowledge of English, and most Greeks are delighted to find a visitor making stabs at speaking Greek, even if they are not very successful. The Greeks do not ridicule you for making mistakes: they themselves have a hard time with Greek spelling and the complicated grammar. Whatever you can manage, guide book in hand, will be welcomed.

In addition to pronouncing every single letter, you should remember that stress plays a very important role in Modern Greek. When you learn a Greek word, you should learn where the stress falls at the same time. Note that each Greek word has a single stress, marked with an accent.

Greek is also an inflected language, and noun and adjective endings change according to gender, number and case. Case endings, the rules governing them and the conjugation of Greek verbs are beyond the scope of a guide and the needs of holidaymakers.

Pronunciation

There are only five vowel sounds: a is pronounced as in English 'pat'; e is as in 'red'; i as in 'bid'; o is like the vowel sound in standard English 'more'; and u is as in 'pull'. The letter y here is always pronounced as in 'yes', not as in 'why' or in 'silly'.

The letter 's' in this guide is always pronounced 's', never as 'z'. The sound represented here as th is always pronounced as in 'thin', not 'that'; note that the first sound in 'that' is represented by dh.

The only difficult sounds are h, which is pronounced like the 'ch' in Scottish 'loch', and gh, which has no equivalent in English, but you can try

producing it by pronouncing the 'ch' in 'loch' and humming at the same time! If that doesn't work, just pronounce it "g" as in "get".

Numbers

one	*éna* (neuter)/
	énas (masc.)/*mya* (fem.)
two	*dhyo*
three	*tría* (neuter)/
	tris (masc. and fem.)
four	*tésera*
five	*pénde*
six	*éxi*
seven	*eptá*

eight	ohtó
nine	enéa
ten	dhéka
eleven	éndheka
twelve	dhódheka
thirteen	dhekatría/dhekatrís
fourteen	dhekatéseris
	etc. until twenty
twenty	íkosi
twenty-one	íkosi éna (neuter and masc.)
	íkosi mya (fem.)
thirty	triándha
forty	sarándha
fifty	peníndha
sixty	exíndha
seventy	evdhomíndha
eighty	ogdhóndha
ninety	eneníndha
one hundred	ekató
one hundred and fifty	
	ekatopeníndha
two hundred	dhyakósa (neuter)
three hundred	trakósa (neuter)
four hundred	tetrakósa (neuter)
one thousand	hília (neuter)

Days of the Week

Monday	dheftéra
Tuesday	tríti
Wednesday	tetárti
Thursday	pémti
Friday	paraskeví
Saturday	sávato
Sunday	kyriakí
yesterday	htes
today	símera
tomorrow	ávrio

Greetings

Hello	yásas (plural/polite)
	yásou (sing./familiar)
	ya (abbreviated)
Good day	káliméra
Good evening	kalispéra
Good night	kaliníhta
How are you?	ti kánete?
	(plural/polite)
	ti kánis? (singular/familiar)

fine, and you? (in response)	
	kalá, esís?
pleased to meet you	
	héro polí (formal)

Getting Around

yes	ne
no	óhi
ok	endáxi
please	parakaló
thank you	efharistó
very much	pára polí
excuse me	sygnómi
I'm sorry	me syghoríte
it doesn't matter	
	dhenbirázi
it's nothing	típota
certainly/yes	málista
Can I..?	bóro na..?
When?	póte?
Where is..?	pou íne..?
Do you speak English?	
	xérete angliká?
What time is it?	
	ti óra ine?
What time will it leave?	
	ti óra tha fíghi?
I want	thélo
here/there	edhó/ekí
small/large	mikró/meghálo
good/bad	kaló/kakó
hot/cold	zestó/krío
bus	leoforío
ship/boat	karávi, plío
ferry	feribót
bike/moped	podhílato/mihanáki
car	aftokínito
ticket	isitírio
road/street	drómos/odhós
beach	paralía
sea	thálassa
church	eklisía
ancient ruin	arhéa
centre	kéndro
square	platía

Hotels

hotel	xenodhohío
Do you have a room?	

	éhete éna dhomátio?
d like...	tha íthela...
single/double (with double bed)	
	éna monó/dhipló
twin-bed	éna dhíklino
ath/shower	bányo/dous
ot water	zestó neró
ed	kreváti
neet	sendóni
ey	klidhí
ntrance	ísodhos
xit	éxsodhos
oilet	toualéta
omen's	yinekón
nen's	ándron
ne bill	to loghariazmó
ome in!	embrós!

Shopping

tore	maghazí/katástima
iosk	períptero
pen/shut	anihtó/klistó
ost office	tahidhromío
tamp	grammatósimo
etter	grámma
nvelope	fákelo
elephone	tiléfono
ank	trápeza
narket	agorá
lave you..?	éhite..?
s there..?	éhi..?
his	aftó (neuter)
low much does it cost?	
	póso káni?
t's (too) expensive	
	ine (polí) akrivó
low much?	póso?
low many?	pósa?

Food

rní	lamb
hirinó	pork
kotópoulo	chicken
keftédhes	meatballs
osári	fish
barbóunia	red mullet
kalamarákia	squid
htapódhi	octopus
asoláda	stewed white beans
domátes	tomatoes

melidzánes	aubergines
patátes	potatoes
tyrí	cheese
psomí	bread
aláti	salt
pipéri	pepper
ládhi	olive oil
avghá	eggs
mílo	apple
stafília	grapes
portokáli	orange

Emergencies

help!	voíthia!
doctor	yiatrós
hospital	nosokomío
pharmacy	farmakío
police	astinomía

Further Reading

Other Insight Guides

Other Insight Guides highlight destinations in this region. Titles include Greece, Greek Islands, Cyprus, Turkey, Istanbul and the Turkish Coast. They each run at well over 300 pages and include full-colour photographs and maps plus a comprehensive listings section, in addition to complete coverage of sights and attractions.

Other titles in the Insight Pocket series are Athens, Corfu and Crete. Like this Pocket Guide to Rhodes, they include suggested itineraries, all plotted on a large fold-out map, as well as sections on history and culture, eating out, shopping and nightlife. A third series of guidebooks, Insight Compact Guides, designed to be on-the-spot reference guides, includes Greece, Crete and Rhodes.

Maps

Insight Fleximaps are a series of fold-out laminated maps, which are noted for their clear cartography and durability. Titles include Athens, Corfu, Crete and Greek Islands.

Index

Notes

Acknowledgments

Cover Design	**Klaus Geisler**
Cartography	**Berndtson & Berndtson**
Photography by	**Presto Press** *and*
Cover	**J. Miller, Robert Harding Picture Library**
8/91	**Plerre Couteau**
24, 31	**John Decopoulos**
23	**Guglielmo Galvin**
5, 40, 67	**Chris Jones**
23, 30, 53r, 55	**D and I Mathioulakis**
12	**National Archaeological Museum**
16	**V Sekellarides**
17	**M Stournara**
13, 14,	**M Toubis**
2/3	**Bill Wassman**

ENGLISH EDITION

Editor	**Maria Lord**
Updaters	**Stephanie Ferguson, Jonathan Abery, Michele Crawford, Paul Hellander**

INSIGHT
Pocket Guides

Insight Pocket Guides pioneered a new approach to guidebooks, introducing the concept of the authors as "local hosts" who would provide readers with personal recommendations, just as they would give honest advice to a friend who came to stay. They also included a full-size pull-out map. Now, to cope with the needs of the 21st century, new editions in this growing series are being given a new look to make them more practical to use, and restaurant and hotel listings have been greatly expanded.

Also from Insight Guides...

Insight Guides is the classic series, providing the complete picture with expert and informative text and stunning photography. Each book is an ideal travel planner, a reliable on-the-spot companion – and a superb visual souvenir of a trip. 193 titles.

Insight Maps are designed to complement the guidebooks. They provide full mapping of major destinations, and their laminated finish gives them ease of use and durability. 85 titles.

Insight Compact Guides are handy reference books, modestly priced yet comprehensive. The text, pictures and maps are all cross-referenced, making them ideal books to consult while seeing the sights. 119 titles.

NOTES